FULFILLED?

How to Land a Job that Aligns

with Your Purpose

by

Wasim Hajjiri

Fulfilled? How to Land a Job that Aligns with Your Purpose

Wasim Hajjiri
San Diego, CA
Wasimhajjiri@gmail.com

Ordering Information:
Special discounts are available on quantity purchases by corporations, associations, educational institutions, and others. For details, contact Wasim Hajjiri above.
Printed in the United States of America
First Edition
ISBN 978-1-5136-9049-0

Publisher: Winsome Entertainment Group LLC

TABLE OF CONTENTS

CHAPTER 1

Got Fulfillment?

Success without fulfillment is the ultimate failure.

—Tony Robbins

What Does Fulfillment Actually Mean?

If you ask someone how they are doing and their answer is "not so bad," does that mean "bad" is their median? How many people feel a sense of fulfillment in their lives? The answer lies within their sense of purpose and whether or not their job brings them fulfillment.

Think about the jobs you have held in your life. Go back to your childhood chores, whether it was washing your dad's car or helping your mom wash the dishes. What was fulfilling about those tasks? Perhaps serving others and making their lives better was fulfilling, or perhaps it was that 50 cents an hour you received.

Now think about your first part-time or full-time job. Was the only fulfillment you experienced getting a paycheck? Do you remember watching the clock, waiting for that magic moment when you could clock out?

What does "job fulfillment" really mean? Job fulfillment simply means you are in a workplace environment that allows you to demonstrate and develop your best talents. Furthermore, people are more fulfilled when their careers fit their temperaments. An introvert might be happy sitting quietly at their desk without interruptions. This person may not do well in a sales job, where a more extroverted person would shine.

The late Steve Jobs, the founder of Apple, spoke about the importance of following your passions when he said that every single day, he woke up, looked in the mirror, and asked himself, "If today were the last day of my life, would I want to do what I am about to do today? And whenever the answer has been 'No' for too many days in a row, I know I need to change something."

At a minimum of 40 hours a week, added up over a lifetime, the majority of our lives are going to be spent at our jobs, so it is extremely important for us to build our work around the things we love and enjoy. It is just as important that your workplace has a culture aligned with your own personal values and where employees are treated with respect and appreciation. Company culture is a crucial aspect of job fulfillment.

Sometimes the company culture may matter more than the salary. If you are in an oppressive environment, no matter what you are doing, you will not be happy. On the other hand, if it's an atmosphere in which you feel respected and loved and it fits your own personal vision, it might be a better fit in the long term, even if it pays less.

What if you want to seek a more fulfilling job? It's time to do some research. Let's say your dream would be to work at Facebook (which was recently renamed Meta). You want to truly discover what the culture is like behind the myth. Do a Google search and learn about Facebook's corporate culture. You may discover a treasure trove of insight into their culture through employee reviews.

What if you want to have more of a voice in the company? In that case, a start-up might be a better fit than an established company where your voice could be more insignificant.

Many times, finding the right job is like finding the right romantic relationship. Sometimes it is a love affair that will last forever. Other times, it is just a stepping stone to something better.

After years of working with hundreds of job seekers, I've been able to summarize their typical experiences into four scenarios when it comes to seeking overall fulfillment.

Scenario 1: You want a completely different career

For many of us, our lives are tapestries of things we love to do and things we need to do. When you feel the inner calling to pursue a new career, it may be because it is time to follow a new path and expand your self-knowledge and skills. In most cases, you will need additional training. In the long run, it is worth it, because what you do every day results in your general happiness.

I met one of my clients, Bob, on LinkedIn. He is a very accomplished tech executive with more than 20 years of coding and app development experience. Bob was making around $200K on average as a base salary. He was a brilliant, extremely marketable candidate, and he was in high demand from companies. He was getting interviews left and right.

After getting laid off due to the COVID-19 pandemic, he spent nearly eight months looking for a new job. He had interview after interview, and nothing was working.

I asked him to take me through what was happening in these interviews. He said, "Every time I go in fully prepared and relaxed, answer all the questions, and then I either get ghosted or rejected." We started working together for about two weeks so he could hone his interview skills.

He became much more confident and prepared, and when he had an upcoming interview the next week, he was 1,000 percent ready to rock and roll. He went in and absolutely nailed it, and within a week, they sent him an initial offer letter! Finally, after all that time, he got it!

I gave him a call to congratulate him. "Hey, Bob! You got the dream job at the dream company! How do you feel?" There was an awkward silence before he responded. "I'm okay," he said in a despondent tone.

"What's wrong Bob? Isn't this what you wanted?"

We talked for about 30 minutes, and he finally spilled the beans. "Wasim, I am not happy with my career. This is not what I love to do."

I was in complete shock. "What?!?" He explained to me that ever since he was a kid, he'd always loved real estate. His dad was a successful agent and always took him on ride-alongs as he did his work. He fell into being a software engineer due to "societal and family expectations" because it is a very lucrative and stable career. He had excelled all his life but really never felt fulfilled. Now, he had reached a point where he was fed up and wanted to make a change. I finally understood why he couldn't land a job for more than eight months by himself: subconsciously, he really didn't want the jobs he was applying for.

Bob was terrified. "Wasim, I've put 20 years into this career. How in the world can I shift into real estate and feed my family by starting from zero?"

We talked about it for two hours and finally came up with a plan. I told him to take the offer and work at the job while we started working on getting his real estate license ASAP. Bob brightened up at the idea and was ready to make that change.

This meant he would be working about 60 hours a week and still need to make time for family and real estate. It was not an easy prospect at all, and he had all the doubts and fears you can imagine.

Fortunately, he had me as his coach to guide him through the process. Even though he was exhausted, Bob's entire life changed when he started to work toward shifting his career to real estate. He woke up with a brand-new fire to do his work and showed up as a completely different person to his family. I even had a conversation with his wife about how much he had changed within a short period of time.

Within a few short months, Bob was able to get his license and started working in real estate on the weekends (after 60-hour work weeks). He became the one of the best agents in his firm within the first six months, and he was the happiest and most fulfilled he'd ever been in his entire career!

I got in touch with him at the end of that year, and he was making enough money to quit his job and was doing real estate full-time!

Scenario 2: You love your company but want to be in a different department

You may feel comfortable with your company's corporate culture, but you want to advance your skills or explore new aspects of the business. If you meet with Human Resources, they can give you a better idea of how you can switch positions. This also may require some internal training.

The experience of one of my clients, Suzie, provides a perfect example. Suzie was an amazing project manager with more than a decade of experience working at top tech companies. At that time, she was working with Google. She was an incredibly talented leader, and her team members and managers loved her. Suzie loved the company and was one of the few people I worked with who was truly fulfilled in their work. In her case, it was mostly because of the great company culture she was in.

But there was something missing for Suzie.

Suzie was overworked. She was working 60–80 hours every single week, including weekends. She barely spent any time with her spouse and family, and she was feeling the negative impact on her work-life balance.

We spoke for more than an hour to understand what kind of changes she wanted to make.

She wanted to stay at Google as a project manager but wanted to lead a different project in a completely different department.

Obviously, this is easier said than done. People facing this type of situation are often plagued by doubt and worry. "What if I lose my job here if I ask to move to another department?" "They might

6

pay me less." "I don't even know who to talk to." "I worked so hard to get this position. What if I fail the interviews and they don't like me anymore?" "I can't leave my team and manager. They are counting on me."

Suzie had these perfectly normal types of fears and really doubted it could be done.

Fortunately, she had a great relationship with her boss, who was also an amazing leader. (This is one reason I always tell my clients to build strong relationships with their teams and bosses).

We started there. Suzie and I practiced her pitch—what to say and how to ask her boss to allow her to move to another department. We did our homework, and she had the full details: department, project, short- and long-term plan/goals, what salary range she wanted, and how many hours per week she wanted to work. There is immense power when you ask for what you want because most people are too afraid to! We even planned out what she was going to tell her team members, one by one.

The next step was to get over her fears and mentally prepare herself to make the move. We worked hard on transforming her mentality, and within a month, she was ready to rock and roll!

She first talked to her team members, who were all very supportive but sad to lose her as a boss. Then she set up a meeting with her manager. She went in and nailed it!

The manager put in a good word for her and was able to get her an interview in the department she wanted to work in.

For a full week, we prepared for the interview until she was 1,000 percent ready. She went in and got the job!

Now, Suzie is working normal 40-hour weeks on the project she was extremely passionate about, and the best part was rebuilding her relationship with her family, which made her even happier and more fulfilled!

Scenario 3: You love what you do but you want to be in a different industry

Many occupations are applicable in multiple industries. For instance, if you have great skills in human resources, those same skills will be useful in a variety of industries. You may be more interested in human resources for hospitals instead of HR at a manufacturing company.

Let's talk about Jessica, a sales manager with more than 12 years of experience working in the tech industry. She always had an easy time finding jobs because she stuck to one industry and did not change. If you are in sales, you understand how important that is.

But there was a problem. She was miserable. She hated going to work and had no fulfillment whatsoever.

You may be thinking, *Well, perhaps she was not being paid enough*, but this was not the case at all. She made six figures for the bulk of her career, so money was not an issue.

The first time we met, I talked to her for an hour and got nothing. "Is it the pay?" "Is it the company?" "Is it the job title?"

None of the above. I told her to do the following: Go on a vacation that upcoming weekend and disconnect completely. Unplug from all technology and bring a notepad and a pen.

I told her to go lie on the beach, close her eyes, completely relax, and, while she was lying on the soft white sand, focus on the sound of the ocean while she envisioned the perfect job and a typical day at work.

The Monday after that weekend, I woke up and found three missed calls and two texts from her.

"WASIM, please call me! I figured it out!"

I called, and her energy and excitement was through the roof! She talked passionately about her ideas for more than 30 minutes. Her joy was contagious, and a huge smile swept across my face.

She now knew what she wanted! Jessica is very passionate about the medical field creating products that improve the health of people around the world. Cancer research was especially close to her heart because she had lost a family member who had battled cancer for years.

So now, it was time to build a plan for her to transition into a completely new industry. She was afraid that because she was moving into a new industry with no experience, no one would hire her. She also worried about a potential salary cut that may come with a new position. As you can see, just as with all the other stories, we will always have fears and doubts. That's part of what makes us human.

Every job seeker experiences self-doubt and fear. As a result, we play the same narrative over and over in our heads to shield us from the pain of potential failure. Jessica did the same, continuing to tell herself that "I don't have enough industry experience."

The most critical step is to get rid of your negative stories for good! We got rid of those fears and got her ready to make the next big move. Jessica still had 12 years of experience, regardless of the industry. With the right job search strategy, she could get the same job—maybe with a little less pay, but the commission structure could always be negotiated.

I worked with her on improving her mindset, and we went full force into the job search. Within two months, she had landed an amazing offer at a cancer research company with an even higher pay than she had before!

Scenario 4: You do not want a job; you want to start your own business

This scenario could be more challenging if you need some start-up capital. This might require that you save money working at your full-time job while simultaneously beginning the planning stages for your business. In certain industries, you may be able to tap into your network and leverage those relationships.

This scenario is completely relatable to my own transition from engineering into business. The most important thing is to start small and take baby steps. Perhaps your goal is to operate a business as a musician, artist, writer, painter, or coach. Whatever the idea may be, the amazing thing is that there are others who have done it successfully before you.

There is no need to reinvent the wheel. You can simply learn from what they did and customize it to your own style. Google is your best friend here! Simply search for phrases such as "How to write a book" or "How to start a business as a chef," and you will find hundreds of *free* books, articles, resources, and mentorship programs—literally *everything* you need. *Do not* try to make up things on your own. I made that mistake before, and it stings, so don't do it.

As I mentioned in Chapter 1, when I decided to move from engineering into coaching, I also had all the doubts and fears in the world: "I can't do this." "What if I fail?" "I've put so many years of my life into engineering. Why leave a stable, lucrative job?" But just like Bob in the first scenario, I really wasn't happy or fulfilled. I had to make a change.

The best thing I did was this: I kept my current job and took baby steps toward starting my own business. The first step was getting my MBA degree to really dive deep into the business world and shift from a technical mindset to a business mindset. Then I broke down all the areas I needed to learn about—coaching, sales, marketing, scaling, etc.—and I found a mentor in each area who helped me get the results I needed.

Starting any business is not easy, and you need to be able to take the failures and punches in the face along the way, just like anything else, such as finding a new job.

Now I'm not suggesting you get an MBA degree, but remember the power of the internet. Google it. Start there and build your way, step by step. With the right kind of mentorship and guidance, you can start any successful business, just like thousands have done before you!

My Personal Search for Fulfillment

I was born and raised in Jordan. In the Jordanian Arabic culture, there is an expectation that children will aspire to prestigious occupations and make a lucrative living. I come from a big family. I have five brothers and three sisters, all older than me. Because I was the youngest, my parents expected the most from me, even though most of my siblings ended up in high-level professional careers. I remember being told over and over to pick one of three major careers: engineer, doctor, or lawyer. The pressure from my parents and society left me with little time to think about what I truly wanted. I was expected to dive into one of those professions right after graduating from high school.

I was not sure what would fulfill me. I never really had the chance to think about what it would be like to follow one of my passions without considering how it could provide a good living for me. I just followed the wish of my father to be the pride of the family.

I began to create a narrative in my head that I could come to the United States—California, specifically—and become a tech tycoon. I always loved technology, and ever since I was a kid, I was a video gamer. I was always fascinated by computers. I liked to pick them apart and learn what was inside them, so I convinced myself I would go into electrical engineering.

Then reality sank in. Even though I was an awesome video gamer and could dissect a computer and put it back together, I had one challenge: I was not the ideal student. My grades were very low, not because of my intelligence but because I was a troublemaker. I was a rebel.

You would think a computer geek would be very introverted, but I was the opposite. I always loved people and working around them. I thrived in environments where I could mingle and be social, which is very, very different from the stereotypical engineer.

As I reached my junior year in high school, I realized I was not on the right path for success. I kept hearing my father's voice in my head. He was fixated on me getting into Princess Sumaya University for Technology, one of the most prestigious universities for studying technology. My dad would sit me down and lecture me about how Bill

Gates is one of the investors for this university. It has a worldwide accreditation, and I could get a job anywhere in the world. Somehow, that thought inspired me more than anything. I felt I had a vision and a goal to get accepted into the school, make my father proud, and look good in front of my siblings.

In a way, the superficial belief that I would be a tech tycoon if I went to this university motivated me to turn things around. The dream of being fulfilled through making money forced me to buckle down, and I worked day and night to raise my grades. In the last year of high school, I devoted all my time to studying to prove I could achieve anything I put my mind to and get accepted into the university.

The day I got my acceptance letter to the Princess Sumaya University for technology to study electrical engineering, I walked around with such pride, but I had no idea what I'd gotten myself into until classes started. It was extremely challenging. Actually, it was hard as hell. It was great that they had top professors from all around the world, but I found it extremely challenging to keep up with the curriculum. Yet I kept that vision of being a California tech tycoon and making my father proud in the back of my mind. That passion pushed me into a mindset of deep discipline for five years.

During my senior year, I was required to complete a graduation project based on creating an idea that would have a global impact. My idea was to create a system for auto theft protection. For the first time, I saw how electrical engineering contributes to the advancement of people's lives. It helped me see there were ways to innovate and further the progress of civilization. It gave me hope that I was embarking on a career that would bring me fulfillment beyond financial success.

I'll never forget the day when I presented my graduation project in front of the very professors who had intimidated me at first. There they were, eager to experience my presentation, when the door opened. My father walked in, went to the back of the room, and sat down. As I glanced at him, I saw him nod his head, and I could read his mind: "My son, the engineer." For a moment, I felt a deep sense of joy from knowing I had fulfilled his dream, and I knew there were more dreams ahead for me.

Fulfilling My American Dream

After I graduated, my father told me over and over that with my engineering degree, I could get a job anywhere in the world, and while I was on a short vacation in New York City, he inspired me to cancel my ticket back home to Jordan and stay in the US to pursue my dream job. My mother was a bit shocked when I told her I was going to move to the US, get a job, and build a new life. The idea that I did not have a job lined up in the US but I was moving there anyway did not sit well with her. That is when I realized a big part of my dream as an electrical engineer was to move to California, even if I didn't have a plan. I realized that true fulfillment for me was more than just a job. It was a lifestyle.

When you know in your heart what you need to feel fulfilled, you need to blast through your fears and uncertainty and trust that you will find your way. After six months of struggle and perseverance, I was able to land my dream job at Qualcomm, a major US technology company. I specialized in telecommunications, and my job was to work on developing and testing the microchips in iPhones and Android phones. I remember how proud my father was that I was one of the engineers behind some of the technology in the mobile phone he held in his hand.

Yet there was an emptiness inside me. I found myself isolated in a lab from morning to night, glued to my computer. I remembered how I used to thrive around people. I saw myself surrounded by introverts who would rather eat lunch at their computers than hang out and explore bigger things in the world. Suddenly, it hit me: even though I had what appeared to be my dream job, working in a dream company where it was extremely challenging to get a position, living in the country I dreamt of living in, something was missing.

I finally realized I was not happy and not getting any fulfillment from the type of work I was doing. Day in, day out, I was just doing the same thing over and over. It was sucking my soul away. I felt I had to make some kind of change because I had lost the motivation to go to work with enthusiasm, and I was just doing the bare minimum. It was not a pleasant experience at all.

However, one of the most exciting things for me was the leadership aspect of the job.

Anytime I had the opportunity to lead a project or a team, I would find myself becoming excited by the prospect of giving presentations or speaking in public. I absolutely loved it. This was one of the things that fulfilled me.

I decided in order for me to make a change, I needed to step into a leadership position. I would have to make a career move that was more aligned with leading projects, working with people, and giving presentations. I started investigating opportunities to be more engaged with various groups. This led me to realize I needed to move ahead in my career. I decided to enroll in the MBA program at the University of California San Diego (UCSD), which is one of the top universities in the world.

It made sense for me to gain business knowledge so I'd have more options: move into another department, make a complete career change, or even start my own business, which was always in the forefront of my mind.

But I did not want to jump into anything for which I didn't have a foundation of knowledge. An MBA degree made a lot of sense because it combined most aspects of business and I could specialize in my areas of interest: leadership, innovation, and entrepreneurship. While I was in the MBA program, I woke up one day with an amazing idea that was about to change my entire life.

Making Your Own Path

I had learned from my own experience how difficult it is to be a new engineering graduate searching for a job. I decided it would be a great asset to create a service or product that helps engineers land their dream jobs and make that whole process easier for them.

I joined a lot of different entrepreneurship programs that help students with their business ideas. They offered numerous opportunities to enter competitions in which you could win cash, prizes, and resources, with the possibility of raising capital to invest in your business.

I knew that to achieve a sense of fulfillment in my career, I needed to assure myself that I would not end up as a failure. I listened carefully to the words of motivational experts as they drove home the importance of replicating the strategies of successful people.

I learned a long time ago that the fastest way for me to learn anything was to learn from the best. This inspired me to join mentorship programs in which I could get guidance from the experts in each of the different fields I was interested in: sales, marketing, innovation, and broader PR products. Fortunately, the school offered a lot of help in building these connections through its affiliate network of top companies.

The school really helped me get connected with the right people and enabled me to build a successful business. I started with marketing, and I got in touch with one of the best professors who taught marketing. He was open to mentoring me and sharing what he knew about online and offline marketing, how to identify target markets, and ways to reach those markets. My passion for learning was unstoppable. I reached out to the most successful people I knew. I learned the most cutting-edge sales strategies from one of the best sales executives I knew.

If I had tried to reinvent the wheel or do everything by myself without proper guidance, I could have ended up behind the eight ball. My mentors enabled me to accelerate exponentially and saved me months and months of figuring out things by myself in the final stages of building out the career coaching business that is now one of my sources of fulfillment.

To build out my idea and scale it, I joined an incubator, which is an extensive entrepreneurship program that provides you with resources to build your business: a leadership team, more mentors, more guidance. I was there for more than eight months. They also helped me write my first book, which talks about my journey of moving from Jordan to the United States.

It took years of hard work, sacrifice, and many failures, but I was finally able to create a successful and sustainable business. I now offer multiple services, including executive/career coaching, public speaking, and more. After many years of being in business, I have learned a lot about the job market and how to help job seekers land jobs, and that is why I decided to put it all together in this second book. Talk about joy and fulfillment! As we all know, the journey of life has many ups and downs. I failed many times in different circumstances, but because of the support and advice I received from so many amazing people, I was able to push through and succeed.

CHAPTER 2

Defining Your Dream Job

Every day can look like your ideal day if you do something ideal.

—Richie Norton

Articulating Your Dream Job

So many times, we hear people fantasizing about their dream jobs. For some, the dream centers on the perks of a nice office with a gym and great food. For others, it is the freedom to primarily work from home, except for in-person meetings. For most, a dream job challenges you, brings out your best, and helps you evolve.

The first piece of advice I give my clients is this: if you cannot articulate what your dream job is, you may never find it.

The first step is to simply have an idea of what you want. Go in initially with an understanding of your interests.

Now it's time to build a vision for the new job. Let's live in la-la land for a second here and ditch all the doubts.

What would a typical day in this new job look like for you, from the moment you wake up until the end of the day? What type of teams do you enjoy working with? How do you see yourself thriving? What's the personality type of the boss or manager you see yourself working with? Give that some thought. And then finally, would you rather be traveling to an office or working remotely from home? Build a beautiful image of this dream job that will inspire you to work hard for it every day.

Step 1: The details of the job

Define the types of roles, companies, and salary that you are interested in.

Example: I want a software engineering/architect/programming lead role at Facebook/Google/Amazon/LinkedIn/HP with a $100K salary and an amazing compensation package (stock options, bonuses, etc.)

Step 2: The timeline to land the job

Set a definite date for when you want to start the job.

Example: Monday, February 28th, 2022 (or "within six months")

Step 3: The vision for the new job

Create a beautiful image of this new job (remember that we are still in la-la land).

Example: I see myself waking up every morning, fired up and excited to go to work. I go into a beautiful office with an amazing view, and I am surrounded by a group of fantastic people. My boss is genuine, supportive, and nice. My team members are on fire, and we have great synergy. The culture is aligned with my values, and I feel a deep sense of fulfillment. At the end of the month, I am excited to receive my paycheck because I'm getting paid the type of salary that I feel I'm worth.

Personally, the way I envisioned my future job was 50 percent remote work and 50 percent in the office. My ideal workplace environment was in a high-rise building in the middle of the city with a view that overlooks the entire city skyline. I saw myself doing something I am passionate about and that makes me feel like I'm making a difference. Every single day, I feel like I'm making the world a much better place.

You are probably thinking, *This all sounds nice, but I have a vision for my job and failed at getting it. I don't believe this can happen for me.* Every time I talk to people about building a new vision, the first thing they tell me is, "Okay, well, I had this dream, and I had an idea of what I wanted to do, but I never got it, so I settled for this job."

Yes, all of that may be true, but that is in the *past*. We are now starting a new page in your job search, and with all the tools you'll learn in this book, you'll be able to turn that vision into reality. I have helped hundreds of people do this, with amazing results.

When you have the right type of mindset and a solid strategy in place, this will all become very easy. Most people struggle with looking for a job, so you are not alone. Again, that was in the past; now get ready for an exciting future!

Now let's switch out of la-la land before hopping on to the next section. While this vision looks and sounds great, the journey will not be easy. In Chapter 5, I talk extensively about how to deal with rejection and failure. It is part of the journey, whether we like it or not, but when you learn how to deal with the negatives, your life becomes easier.

My client Paul found success when he was finally able to define and visualize his dream job. When I first started working with Paul, he was completely lost in his search for a new job transition. He was a senior developer with more than 25 years of experience, and he did not know where to go. The first thing we did was write down his vision for his dream job. He wrote, "$200,000 base salary, working in a culture similar to a start-up, full-on remote, and a location close to New York City so I can be close to my family."

We worked together for more than six months, and Paul went through many good interviews, some not-so-good interviews, and even a few failed offers. At one point, he almost gave up and didn't want to continue. I kept him on track mentally and always pushed him to keep going. At the end of the period, he got not one but three different offers! He picked the one that resonated with his needs the most.

After he signed the contract for his new job, we went back to the vision he had written down for his dream job. They were extremely similar, and that completely blew his mind! This is the power of having an idea of what you want.

The Three Pillars of Your Dream Job

Now that you have a basic idea of your dream job, it's time to dig a little bit deeper. These are the three pillars that will give you some direction so you can pick the right company to work for.

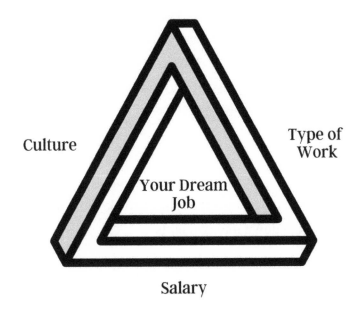

Culture

Type of Work

Your Dream Job

Salary

Company culture

In the first chapter, I talked about fulfillment. This simply means your job fulfills your personal and professional needs—not superficially, but in a meaningful and significant way. This deep fulfillment is achieved when the company you are working for has values that are aligned with your own; their mission statement is aligned with your own personal mission statement. Thus, a critical factor of job fulfillment is rooted in company culture.

I want you to take a moment and think about all the jobs you've had. Honestly, how many of those jobs had a culture that produced a sense of true fulfillment? What even *is* true fulfillment?

It starts with believing your innate talents can fully blossom through your work. It feels like waking up with the sunrise and being filled with joyful anticipation for another day to serve and create in your own authentic way.

Job fulfillment also includes being a part of a culture that is supportive as well as challenging. A strong company culture will inspire you and others at the workplace to grow. You need to do a little self-inquiry and company research to assure their values are aligned with your own values and mission.

Type of work

Now that you have an idea of the company culture you want to be in, the second thing to consider is the type of work you will be doing. This can be broken down into two parts:

1) Industry

You might have worked in a specific industry and want to transition to a different one, or you may be starting out fresh. Regardless of your area of expertise and education (sales, marketing, engineering, project management, etc.) or your level of experience (junior/mid/senior), you have to be in an industry that is exciting for you.

According to the US Bureau of Labor Statistics, there are 69 industries in the US (e.g., information technology, health care, energy, financial, real estate, etc.). Thus, the opportunities are seemingly endless. Now, some of you might be thinking, *I've been in the same industry for 10 years. I can't change it now*! Well, of course you can! You might take a little pay cut, but you have to be in an industry you're excited about, and the strategies in this book can be used in any industry!

As I mentioned earlier, I absolutely love technology, and that's the industry I've been in for more than a decade now. This passion goes back to my childhood; I loved computers, and I was always interested in the new technologies that evolved and positively impacted our lives.

Do a Google search, find out what types of industries are exciting for you, and narrow down the list to your top three.

2) Job description

The job description for any role you are interested in will give you an idea of what the day-to-day activities of that position will look like. In the initial stages of the application process, you can also ask the recruiter or hiring manager for more details about what you will be doing on a daily basis. First, you want to make sure you are at least 70 percent qualified for the role before even thinking of applying, and then you need to be sure the job description sounds really exciting for you. We all know jobs are not perfect, but you need to at least be happy with it.

Salary

Now let's talk about salary, which is the last pillar. I have an entire section in Chapter 9 that talks about salary negotiation in detail, but before all that, you need to have an initial idea of the salary you want. This is based on three things:

1) Job title

2) Location

3) Industry

Let's say you are applying for a sales position in California within the IT industry (without a specific company in mind). Go to your best friend, Google, and type in "IT sales salaries in California."

You will find a lot of websites that will give you an idea of the range based on your level of expertise (junior/mid/senior).

In Chapter 9, "How to Nail Interviews," I talk about salary in more detail and effective ways to ask an employer for the salary you want.

Now you have an idea of the three pillars: company culture, type of work, and salary.

Example:

Let's say you are a mid-level software engineer.

Company culture: Start-up (having a voice, open culture)

Type of work: Coding in the languages I love most (e.g., Python, C++)

Salary: $100K–$120K

Now how do you find a company that is aligned with what you are looking for? It comes down to three main things:

1) Alignment of values

2) Researching best companies

3) Company employee benefits

1. Alignment of Values

Having clarity about whether you and your prospective employer share similar values is very important. For instance, if you live a very green lifestyle and you discover the company you are applying for has a poor environmental record, that could be an important factor in your deciding not to work at that company. On the other hand, if you are interviewing for an executive position, you may see this as an opportunity to inspire best practices with a green initiative. This would be a fantastic challenge you could be determined to tackle in your new role. In most cases, accomplishing such change may only be possible on a small scale, as opposed to large infrastructure changes.

Your values could also include finding an open atmosphere that inspires innovation and collaboration, giving you the chance to soar. This is the kind of information you need to gather. For instance, if you are in the software development world, you might want to find a company that employs the Agile methodology. Agile is centered around a type of project management where solutions are discovered through a collaborative approach based on the creation of self-organizing and cross-functional teams, which include clients. The benefits of Agile include improved project predictability and increased flexibility. This leads to better team morale and a more creative environment.

It's very important that the company's values are aligned with your own. So what does that mean? Let's dig deeper.

Before you can find a company culture that is aligned with your own values, you have to first understand what you like. On a perfect day, what is typically your style of work? Do you enjoy working with people or alone? Do you like working on something challenging or something easy and repetitive? Do you like to be innovative, or do you just want to be part of what the company is doing? Do you like to have a voice and present your own ideas, or are you okay with tagging along with other people's ideas?

Ask yourself these questions to get a better idea of what kind of company culture you would personally like to be in. Next, you have to have a very deep understanding of the company you're applying to work for. What exactly are they working on? What are their products or services? What is the purpose behind their work? How are they ethical or unethical? Is their work saving the environment? Is it helping people? Is it changing medicine? This is what will be important for you to understand so you can learn to align your own values with the company, especially if you want to stay long-term.

After you have an idea of what you like, you will find multiple companies that will fit that vision. Think of interacting with these companies as similar to dating. When you date different people, some will like you, and some won't. It's the same when you are interviewing. You do your part to prepare and be ready for the interviews. But in the end, you have to match with the right kind of company. They have to be as invested in you as much as you want to be invested in them. And when it's the right match, it will happen naturally, without being forced and without any pressure.

If one of these is missing, you will not get the fulfillment and the joy you want. It doesn't have to be perfect, but it should at least be close to something you like in terms of culture, the type of work you're doing, and pay that matches what you feel you are truly worth.

2. Researching Best Companies

Discovering if your values are aligned is a great first step. As you deepen your exploration of the company, there are quite a few areas you want to research. You want to understand the company's culture and its leadership. You can do a Google search to get a sense of this from their social media and media profiles. Research articles and white papers so you can wrap your mind around the ideas that shape the company.

LinkedIn ranked the best companies to work for based on the career support they offer to their employees, including promotions, skill development, tenure, employee retention, and employee growth. Amazon came in at number one.

There are three main websites I recommend my clients use for researching companies:

1. Google
2. Wikipedia
3. Glassdoor

Let's say you want to work for Google or Facebook. Simply go on Google.com, Wikipedia, or Glassdoor. Check out the summary of the company, what they're about, the latest articles, and, most importantly, employee reviews. Obviously, it's important to read all the employee reviews, but that's not a deal breaker. You shouldn't base your decision on whether to work at the company solely on employee reviews.

After you get a basic idea of what the company is like from the reviews, there are two more important ways to find out more information. Number one is through the actual interviews. When talking to the recruiter, ask them a lot of questions about the company culture, what it's like to work there, and the people you will be potentially working with. That way, you'll get a lot of information.

The second part is to go on LinkedIn, search for people who work at that company, connect with them, and message them: "Hey James, I'm thinking about working for this company. I wanted to connect with you to get an idea of how it is working there because I'm very excited."

Start connecting with people in the company and ask them questions about what their experience is like working there. You will get a better idea of what the company is all about from the people who are actually working there. Some people will respond, while others will not. It's normal, and it's part of the game.

I understand that you might feel a little bit pushy or plagued with thoughts like *Why am I connecting with these people? Am I bothering them?* I want you to get completely out that fearful mindset and into the mindset of networking, which is simply building organic relationships.

There are so many amazing people in the world waiting for you to connect with them. If you analyze and study successful people, you'll find they are very happy to help others succeed.

Unfortunately, in our society, many of us were raised with the idea that if we ask for help, it shows weakness and will hurt our pride or ego. However, asking for help shows power and authenticity. It shows vulnerability and that we are human beings who need help, and we love to help each other. In order to help each other out, we have to connect. You need to push yourself out of your comfort zone and be open to building genuine relationships with people because you never know what kind of amazing human being can change your life in one day.

I have many great stories about networking. Let me share with you one that changed my life and career within one day.

Years ago, I went to a big fitness expo event. My dream was to meet Arnold Schwarzenegger, the famous bodybuilder, actor, and former California governor. While I was there, I was walking around, and I saw this guy wearing a classic Arnold jacket that I liked. My friend told me, "Go ask him where he got it so we can get you one." I simply walked up to him and said, "Hi."

It turned out this guy trains Arnold Schwarzenegger's son Patrick, and he knows all the celebrities who were on my bucket list to meet, including the legendary Frank Zane. Keep in mind that I did not know this guy, and I didn't even have anything to give him.

Long story short—he opened doors for me to meet celebrities and endorsed my book, and many more doors opened from that simple conversation. He helped me out of the kindness of his heart and completely changed my life. You never know who might change yours.

3. Company Employee Benefits

A 2015 Glassdoor survey revealed people find benefits and perks to be a major factor when considering a job offer. The survey also found 80 percent of employees would choose a strong benefits package over higher pay. As I write this book, one of the most important benefits beyond healthcare insurance is the option to work from home. Depending on the sector, you may be able to work remotely. If you are in a career that requires you to be on-site, you must be assured there is a good package of paid time off and paid family leave.

Employee benefits are a pivotal aspect of your compensation. It's amazing that eight out of 10 people would rather have better benefits than a higher salary—that is a huge, huge number. These benefits can be remote work, travel insurance, stock options, commissions, bonuses, raises, growth opportunities, educational advancement, and more.

It's a matter of what is more important to you on a personal level. Let's say you have a big family and kids, so insurance is more important for you. Or maybe you truly thrive by working remotely versus in an office, so this may be the most important factor for you.

One of my clients, Roger, was a senior project manager. When I dug deep and understood what he truly valued when it came to company benefits, it was the fact that he enjoyed working remotely and excelled in that environment. Working remotely allowed him to spend more time with his family, which means that for him, family is very important. It's not even a matter of how much he is paid. He told me that he would rather get paid $20,000 less but continue to work remotely because, again, that allows him to spend more time with his family instead of wasting precious hours commuting to work.

Be very picky about the benefits you want, and negotiate each of these areas. To get a better idea of how you can get closer to what you enjoy, you can use the same websites I mentioned in the previous section (Google, Wikipedia, and Glassdoor).

CHAPTER 3

Finding Your Inner Strength

What could you do if you valued yourself more?
Whatever you think your worth in life and business, double it.
Then double it again.

—Richie Norton

The Curse of Procrastination

Procrastinate (verb): *to put off intentionally and habitually; to put off*
intentionally the doing of something that should be done.

Do you see yourself as a procrastinator? You may wonder, *What the heck does it really mean to procrastinate?* Generally, someone who would be considered a procrastinator is someone who avoids important tasks in life. That does not necessarily mean the person is lazy, but rather it may be more associated with anxiety. They may really have the intent to do something, but instead they are in the active process of choosing to focus on something else and have several different narratives in their head. When it comes to job searching in a rapidly moving job market, the issue is that as they think the early bird gets the worm. They may avoid or delay taking any action to such a degree they allow opportunities to pass them by. Many times, they will have an excuse.

Here are the most common excuses and antidotes for avoiding important tasks such as your job search:

- "I'll do this tomorrow." Somehow there always seems to be something that needs to get done before you complete that job application. Then the day runs out, and it is one of those unfinished tasks. You may feel guilty and promise yourself you will do it first thing in the morning. Then you wake up, and of course there is an urgent matter, and the job application falls further down the list.

- "I'm too tired to do this now." You may finally get to the job application and then realize you are honestly too tired to do it.

- "It's too hard."

- "I worked too much today, so I'm just going to rest."

- "I'll do this later."

- "I posted my résumé on Indeed and Monster. I'll wait until they contact me."

- "I'll apply for jobs tomorrow, not now. I don't feel like it."

The antidote for "I'll do this tomorrow" is simply to employ the process of stack ordering.

How do you stack order? Create a well-ordered to-do list on which the addition of a new item necessitates the removal of an existing item.

After listening to hundreds of hours of audios, watching countless videos, and reading a ton of books about success, I learned this one simple strategy can easily help you break free of those excuses.

Every time you hear yourself create an excuse for not doing something, make *one* simple, small step toward its achievement *right away*, at that same instant.

Example 1:

You want to apply to 50 jobs today, and your mind says, "Ah, that's too much. I'm tired, blah blah blah ..."

Right away, at that same instant, get your butt out of the chair, walk to your computer or pick up your cell phone, and apply to *one* job. After disproving your hypothesis that "Ah, that's too much," you'll gain amazing momentum. You'll apply to another job, and another, and another. Who knows—you might even do the whole 50!

Example 2:

You gained 15 pounds over the Christmas break, and you decided to work out today. Your mind says, "Ah, it's too hard, and I'm too fat to work out anyway."

Right away, at that same instant, get up, go outside, and walk for 10 minutes. As soon as you finish that, you'll think to yourself, *This is easy. Let me do another 15 minutes*, and you'll end up having completed a 25-minute workout instead of not doing anything at all!

This is just like magic! As you continue to take these little baby steps, you'll be programming your brain to break free from the excuses because you'll be constantly breaking those old patterns. Soon enough, the procrastination will go away, and you'll start taking actions beyond your wildest imagination!

Remember, consistency is key!

Steps to Building Unshakable Confidence

One of the most effective ways to improve your self-image is the deliberate use of positive self-talk. You already talk to yourself. We all do, constantly! But we don't usually listen consciously to our internal dialogue. Sometimes it's negative and holds us back from acting. When you're aware of your own negative self-talk, you can replace those self-defeating thoughts with empowering messages, lifting yourself up and building enormous self-confidence.

You're by yourself most of the day anyway, so it won't matter what other people say about you. What matters is what you say about yourself!

A great example of positive self-talk is Muhammad Ali's famous phrase, "I am the greatest!" He continuously carried that message with him from a young age and became the greatest heavyweight champion of all time.

You're probably thinking, *Okay, positive thinking is nice, but what about the negative thinking that hits me out of nowhere?* Tony Robbins explains this perfectly: "The brain is old and is not designed to make us happy; it's designed to make us survive." This happens to all of us. Doubt and fear come into the mix as well. Your brain starts telling you:

- I'm not good enough for this job.

- I'm going to fail.

- This will never work.

- I suck at applying for jobs, so I might as well stop applying.

- I can't do this.

36

Step 1

Trying to analyze all this in your brain and flip it around might be challenging, so the most effective way to make lasting change is to work on three areas called the Triad:

1) Physiology

2) Focus

3) Language

1) Change your physiology (the way you move your body or "physical state").

Here are just a few ways you can do this:

- A breathing exercise

- A jumping exercise

- An intense walk or training session

- Dance

- A cold shower

- Force a smile and hold it for 30 seconds (it will feel awkward, so you'll laugh)

- Fix your posture, whether you are standing or sitting (back and shoulders straight, chest up)

- Listen to energizing or inspirational music

2) Change your focus.

Shift your focus from negative thoughts to three to five things you're grateful for in your life. Whatever we focus on, we believe.

It might be difficult and feel uncomfortable to shift your focus, but push through and do it. Gratitude is very powerful, and it always beats negative emotions.

Example:

Say your thoughts are focused on how you've been rejected and interviews that turned out badly. When that happens, start thinking about your family, your friends, and your home and how blessed you are to have them.

You'll start to feel better, and your focus will shift away from the negative things that have happened in the past or that could happen in the future. If it doesn't work right away, don't give up. Keep going and think about even more things you're grateful for. It will eventually make you feel better.

3) Change your language.

When you're thinking negatively, most of the things going through your head are framed in a negative, disempowering language.

Example:

Why am I so fat?

Change this question into:

How can I lose weight and get into the best shape of my life?

Step 2

The next set of exercises are designed to help you reprogram your conscious and subconscious mind so you can build new positive thoughts that will replace fear, doubt, and negative self-talk.

Think of five to 10 positive things you can say to yourself as you are going through this amazing journey of applying for your dream job.

Example:

- I am an experienced, valuable employee. Any company will be lucky to have me.

- I have unlimited talents and abilities.

- I am sexy, confident, and unique.

- I am energetic, strong, passionate, and confident, and I can accomplish the impossible.

- I am successful and capable of achieving anything.

- I am wealthy. Everything I dream of is possible.

- I love life and people, and I enjoy the small moments and am grateful for what I have.

Step 3

We all accomplish so much in our lives that we often forget to give ourselves credit for our achievements. Write down all of your accomplishments. These can be very simple, so don't complicate it. You don't have to be a Nobel Prize winner. Everything you do is special and unique. Don't underestimate your power! Every small step you take toward your goals is a huge accomplishment and a big success.

Examples:

- I earned an engineering degree

- I graduated with an MBA degree

- I'm a great son and friend

- I take my mom out every week for one-on-one quality time

- I helped a friend when he needed me most

- I lost 15 pounds

- I won two Olympic gold medals

- I won a USA national gold medal

- I've appeared on TV six times

- I got to 4 percent body fat

- I've traveled to Europe

- I quit smoking

Step 4

In addition to what we've accomplished, we all are different, unique, and beautiful in our own special ways. Write down a list of everything you like about yourself—appearance, personality, intellect—everything you can think of.

Examples:

- My personality

- My friendliness

- My physical appearance

- My style

- My commitment to the gym

- My relationship with my family and friends

- My work ethic

- My passion for life and people

When people ask you about yourself, what do you say? Describe yourself in one simple sentence.

Example: I define myself as *energetic, ambitious, hardworking, and passionate about life and people.*

These simple exercises serve as reminders of who you are and what you represent. Never forget how much you had to go through to get to this point in your life. You have innate talents, unique abilities, and a soul the whole world needs to see. Show them what you are made of!

CHAPTER 4

Branding

If people like you, they will listen to you,
but if they trust you, they'll do business with you.

—Zig Ziglar

Your Personal Values Are Reflected in Your Personal Brand

We have been born into a world of brands. From diapers to beer, we are inundated with advertisements for a plethora of brands. Many of the products and services are similar to their competitors, with one exception: branding.

What is branding? Branding is a way to present a product or service. In your case, *you* are your personal brand.

Your personal brand is reflected in your bio, on your website, and in all the ways you present yourself to the world. In particular, you need to be very conscious of what you post on social media. Your personal pages are exposed to everyone, and your business pages are not all a prospective employer looks at. Before you get extremely political on Facebook or post lots of partying pictures on your Instagram page, be aware that a potential employer can determine a lot about your character from your personal social media.

Building your personal brand is more than looking good for prospective employers. It is a statement about yourself. It can show your expertise through content you create and post. By establishing an online presence with intelligent content, you could gain the winning edge over someone who just has a Facebook page with family pictures. If you do post original content such as a blog, be sure to present your ideas in a digestible way that highlights your key points.

After talking to thousands of job seekers, I've learned the most important brand is not just online and what we mentioned above. It is your own personality and your own mindset. What does that mean? It simply means that every time you pick up the phone and talk to a potential employer, a recruiter, or a hiring manager, *that* is your personal brand—the most important brand we want to double down on and make strong.

Because think about it: When you're applying to any job, there are going to be hundreds and hundreds of people applying to the same job. And most of them might have the exact same résumé or similar résumés as yours, right? So what will define you from all the rest of those people who are applying?

Think about Google. Everyone in the world knows what Google is. There are a lot of other search engines—Yahoo, Bing, etc.—but no one says, "Let's Yahoo it." Personal branding is the same. How can you be the Google amidst all the other people with the exact same experience? If you change your branding, you will appear much more attractive to any potential employer.

Job Search Branding

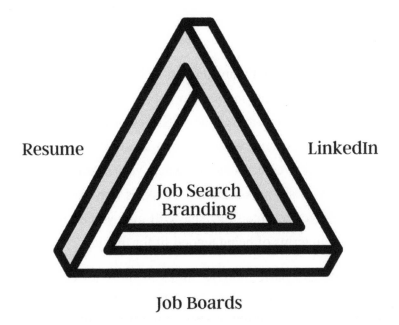

Resume   LinkedIn

Job Search
Branding

Job Boards

When it comes to the job search, your brand = having an ATS-optimized résumé + a magnetic LinkedIn profile + accounts on all the top job boards.

1. How to Optimize Your Résumé Using the ATS

The old days of hiring managers reading your résumé are gone. Nowadays, they use the ATS (Applicant Tracking System), the software 85 percent of companies use to find job candidates. The ATS looks for keywords that convey two main things: key qualifications and key (technical and nontechnical) skills. After more than a thousand calls with job seekers, I learned about 80 percent of them had problems getting interviews because of the ATS, and they didn't even know what it is or how it works.

To find those keywords you need for the ATS, its actually very simple.

Step 1

Let's say you are a project manager. Go on LinkedIn and find three to five jobs you are interested in, but don't apply to them at first. We will use these job descriptions to find the ATS keywords we need. LinkedIn can be a great tool because when you upgrade to the premium edition with the job seeker/career feature, when you scroll down the job description, it will show you the top 10 skills (keywords), what you have, and what you are missing. That will give you an initial idea of where you are in terms of being a good fit for that job.

Now copy and paste the URL links of these jobs into an Excel sheet so you can keep track of them, and we will use them throughout the branding process.

Step 2

There are many websites that will help you with the ATS. My favorite one that I use with all my clients is www.jobscan.co. The basic version is free, and there are many great features you can use if you upgrade to the premium version.

You simply upload your résumé and then copy and paste the information in the job description. It will do all the magic for you, giving you details about how you can build out your résumé, and it shows you what keywords you are missing.

Below is the résumé draft I have used with hundreds of clients, and it scored very high on the ATS after using Jobscan. Whether you are at the entry, middle, or senior level, this will apply in the same way.

James James
Number: 732-865-2889

Email: jamesjames@gmail.com

LinkedIn: linkedin.com/in/jamesjames/

Holmdel, NJ

SUMMARY

Information Security Analyst with over 3 years of combined experience in the Information Security field. Capable of multitasking between a variety of tasks and departments. Experience handling the Cybersecurity training and awareness initiatives for multiple companies. Proven record of successful work regarding pre-audit preparations for various teams and compliance regulations.

SKILLS

Project Management	Leadership	Compliance Assessment
Documentation Writing	Training and Education	Security Controls
Information Security Systems	Data Privacy	Security Systems
OWASP	Risk Analysis	Risk Management
Cloud Service	Operations	Evaluation

JavaScript | Python | Java | C++

Microsoft Office Suite | Microsoft ATA | Metasploit | SolarWinds | Wireshark

Documented Policies and Procedures, including SOX 404, SSAE 16 SoC 1 and 2 reports, and Data Privacy and Protection (i.e. CCPA)

EDUCATION, CERTIFICATIONS, & ADDITIONAL LEARNING

Bachelor of Science (BS), Cybersecurity, Rochester Institute of Technology
August 2014–May 2019

- Honors: RIT Presidential Scholarship, Dean's List

PROFESSIONAL WORK EXPERIENCE

Jr. Security Analyst

Johnson & Johnson

Piscataway, NJ

August 2019–Present

- Conducts various cybersecurity risk assessments on applications and third parties that fall under a variety of compliance requirements, including HIPAA and SOX.

- Assists in several internal and external audits regarding SOX and HIPAA compliance for our applications.

- Creates threat models to identify potential risks that applications may face with their current vulnerabilities to assist in prioritizing the vulnerabilities and their remediation.

- Creates various resources used in cybersecurity training and awareness initiatives for contact center staff, including an awareness video and monthly emails regarding cybersecurity topics.

Pathways Intern

National Park Service

Washington, D.C.

February 2019–May 2019

- Developed a program that functions alongside Google Forms to assist hiring managers in contacting appropriate hiring authorities when searching for prospective employees.

Cybersecurity Intern

Palindrome Technologies

Holmdel, NJ

June 2018–August 2018

- Developed scripts for remotely executing files via SSH to discover network devices and assist in network mapping.
- Presented to management information regarding Distributed Version Control Systems, SSH, and Public Key Cryptography.

Information Security Analyst

Kodak Alaris

Rochester, NY

August 2017–May 2018

- Wrote several company policies and procedures, including the Acceptable Use Policy, Phishing Report Policy, Metasploit Pro Process, and Metasploit Pro Rules of Engagement.
- Assisted other Security team members in completing a company-wide audit for ISO 27001 compliance.
- Completed the pre-audit for ISO 27001 for the company-wide audit and documented current PCI DSS compliance.
- Created and managed the cybersecurity training to be used by the Information Security Team when assigning all US employees with cybersecurity training.

Now go back to those links for the jobs you found in Step 1 and apply the same process to each one.

The premium version makes it easier by uploading up to three URLs, and it performs the scan across all three at the same time.

Step 3

Now your résumé will be ATS optimized and ready to rock and roll. This will significantly increase your chances of landing interviews. We will also use the new résumé to optimize your LinkedIn profile.

LinkedIn is now the number one most-used platform for landing jobs. According to *Forbes*, about 85 percent of all companies use LinkedIn to find job candidates. You want to have a strong presence on LinkedIn starting right now.

2. How To Build a Magnetic LinkedIn Profile

In the previous section, we worked on the résumé, and now it is ATS optimized. We will use it in some parts for LinkedIn.

Your profile is broken down into 10 sections:

1) Dashboard

2) Featured

3) Activity

4) About/Bio

5) Experience

6) Education

7) Volunteer experience

8) Skills and endorsements

9) Recommendations

10) Accomplishments

LinkedIn is always making changes and optimizing their platform, so over time, these might be slightly different. Just as with any other social media platform, the more you fill out in these sections, the better the algorithm works in your favor, which equals more recruiters and hiring managers visiting your profile.

1) Dashboard

This feature is great because it shows you the number of profile visitors per day and who specifically is interested in your background. The premium feature gives you more data and insights.

2) Featured

The first things you want to add to this section are your résumé, cover letter, and any content you feel is important for potential employers to see.

3) Activity

It's always good to stay active and make at least one post per week. It helps boost your visibility and engagement with the people in your network.

4) About/Bio

There are three parts to a successful bio:

1. A short one-paragraph summary that outlines your:

    - Total number of years of experience

    - Areas of expertise

    - Recent accomplishments/awards/key highlights you would like companies to know about

Example:

Ambitious, team-oriented management professional with 20+ years managing and overseeing dynamic work environments and implementing best practice processes and programs to maximize staff productivity. Adept at assessing plans, devising solutions, and streamlining operations to improve bottom-line profitability while supporting the development and launch of corporate sustainability programs.

2. Core Competencies: Tangible and Intangible Skills

   Example:

   - Pre-Sales Strategic Information Consulting

   - Project Management Methodologies

   - Medicaid/Medicare Regulatory Compliance

   - Claims Analysis/Adjudication

   - Healthcare Experience

   - Service-Level Guidelines and Policies

   - Medical Coding

   - Operations Management

   - Standard Operating Procedures (SOP)

   - Claims Billing

3. Key Professional Highlights

   Example:

   - Facilitated Payment Integrity Solutions working with recognized and strategic partners to provide proven fraud detection software and decision support tools for Fraud, Waste, and Abuse

- Applied analytic tool sets for medical claims review/ investigation, medical coding, data mining/analysis, investigative analysis, case tracking/investigation and audit results

- Developed and delivered 100+ healthcare payer BPO solutions/cost models for contracts valued from $2M to $1B

5) Experience

After optimizing your résumé using the ATS (www.Jobscan.co) and using the draft in the previous section, you can copy and paste your job experience as is from the new résumé.

6) Education

Same as number 5.

7) Volunteer experience

If you don't have any volunteer experience, think about doing something small to get rolling. Find ways to add value to your community

8) Skills and endorsements

This is an extremely important section because you can add a lot of the keywords the ATS is looking for here. Let's go back to the sample résumé draft:

SKILLS

Project Management	Leadership	Compliance Assessment
Documentation Writing	Training and Education	Security Controls
Information Security Systems	Data Privacy	Security Systems
OWASP	Risk Analysis	Risk Management
Cloud Service	Operations	Evaluation

JavaScript | Python | Java | C++

Microsoft Office Suite | Microsoft ATA | Metasploit | SolarWinds | Wireshark

Documented Policies and Procedures, including SOX 404, SSAE 16 SoC 1 and 2 reports, and Data Privacy and Protection (i.e., CCPA)

The Jobscan website will really help you narrow these down. If you have any of them missing on your LinkedIn profile, just add them using this list. If your skills are maxed out, you can include them anywhere else, even in the about section (the ATS software will still detect the keywords).

9) Recommendations

I always recommend having at least 3–5 recommendations. Again, the more completely you've filled out your profile, the better the LinkedIn algorithm works for you. Plus, it always looks better when recruiters or hiring managers are looking at your profile and they see that other people recommended you. It adds credibility.

10) Accomplishments

Think about all your personal and professional accomplishments: sports, publications, awards, accolades, grades, courses, patents, publications, etc., and list them here.

3. How To Leverage Job Boards to Boost Your Visibility

In the last two sections, we worked on the résumé and LinkedIn profile. The last part of the puzzle is the job boards. The top 10 job boards used by Fortune 500 companies are:

1. Indeed

2. Monster

3. LinkedIn

4. ZipRecruiter

5. Monster

6. CareerBuilder

7. FlexJobs

8. Google for jobs

9. Lensa

10. Ladders

After you have your résumé ATS optimized, go onto these websites, create profiles, upload your résumé, and make it public. This is a complete game changer and will tremendously boost your visibility for multiple reasons:

1) The ATS software works similarly as SEO (Search Engine Optimization), which simply means that when recruiters and hiring managers are looking for candidates with a background like yours, they also use a Google search. The more profiles you have, the easier it will be for them to find you. Let's say, for example, a recruiter is looking for project managers. Your name will appear much higher on the search list simply because you have your résumé uploaded on multiple platforms.

2) When you have profiles on these websites, recruiters and hiring managers will automatically start to reach out to you whenever they have jobs that match your background. This will increase the number of interviews more than you can ever imagine.

Identifying Your Assets, Characteristics, and Strengths

In the previous sections, we nailed down job search branding. Now let's talk about you and dig into your own personal brand. To present the most captivating and impressive personal brand, you need to take the time and identify what makes you stand out from the rest. What is it about you that is distinct and exceptional?

Let's start with your character and nature. Here is where you need to make a list of your personal values. For instance, if you value truth and integrity, you may want to have your own personal vision statement that reinforces your commitment to these values.

Your assets are your strengths. Sometimes your strengths have not had a proper proving ground. I return to my experience as an engineer while wanting to be a leadership facilitator. When I saw the window of opportunity to lead my team and do presentations, that gave me my first opening to prove how valuable I was in a leadership capacity. Once I saw how natural it was for me to lead and present, I knew my days as a hands-on engineer were numbered.

If you still need some help to discover the specific characteristics of your personality, there is nothing more effective than the Myers-Briggs Type Indicator personality inventory. This test has been used for decades by employers wanting to understand the personality types of their prospective employees. It is based on 16 personality types that result from the interactions among four major categories of preferences: introversion/extraversion, sensing/intuition, thinking/feeling, and judging/perceiving. The conceptual framework of Myers-Briggs is based on psychiatrist Carl Jung's theory.

To break this down for you, let's explore where you are. Are you more action-oriented and love to keep busy, or are you more of a thinking person who enjoys strategizing? When you focus on a problem, do you rely on your intuition, or do you sense it? These nuances may seem subtle, but once you take the test, you will see a fairly accurate picture of your personality and what kind of work is best for your soul.

Another great tool to discover your strengths is the <u>VIA Survey of Character Strengths</u>. It is free, easy, and will give you a good picture of your strengths.

How do you boost your personal brand from within? How do you get more confidence from within? In addition to all these different tests you can take, I want you to ask yourself a simpler question: What do you most love about yourself? What do your friends love most about you?

Is it your kind, genuine heart that helps others when they need you? Is it your strong relationships with others? Or is it your work ethic and your drive? What about the way you show up and get things done? Believe it or not, these are the most important things for you to discover and reflect on because this is what all employers are looking for. I heard a phrase years ago that stuck with me: "Companies invest in people, not in résumés."

Write down this phrase and memorize it. What makes you unique? Is it your personality, energy, essence, and being? These characteristics will differentiate you from all the other candidates and make you the X factor for the companies you are applying for. It's not just your résumé.

Your Magnetic Presence

Visuals are very important. If you don't have a website for your personal brand, consider creating one. Make sure you work with a web designer who captures the style you want to project. Check out the other websites they have built. Also check out the websites of influencers you admire. What is it that attracts you to this person, and how are they presented on their website? Your website will be someone's first impression of you.

If you are looking to have a magnetic social media presence, you should consider video. This can showcase both your presence and your intelligence. If you are looking to get a position where you are speaking professionally, you will need a stellar reel. If you do have a video of yourself speaking that feels authentic and presents the best of you, by all means, use it!

When creating social media profiles, make sure you keep it consistent. Even though your personal social media profiles are not showcases for your professional presence, you want to create a uniform look and feel. Remember, you want to shape an image that will radiate out to the public, and that is how they will perceive you.

Now as a job seeker, the main profile you want to work on is LinkedIn because 80 percent of companies use LinkedIn to hire people.

We already took care of that in the previous section.

Your Affiliation with Influencers and Associations

We are all familiar with the term "guilt by association." How about "admiration by association"? The people you wish to affiliate within social media will be reflected in your personal brand. It is highly recommended to join professional associations as well as community organizations. When a prospective employer sees how active you are in your profession as well as your community, it will give you an edge over someone who does not seem to be involved in much group activity.

You may also consider seeking endorsements from those you admire in your profession. You will first need to make the connections. For example, if you are a big fan of a motivational speaker, find out where they will be speaking, and do your best to meet the person afterward. Ask them if they are open to read something you had published and how you might send it to them, or ask if you can interview them. If you are bold and respectful, you never know what could result.

If you know you won't be able to get in front of this influential person or they do not respond to your invitations, you can always put a quote from the person on your website or use a famous quote from someone you admire.

Put all of this together and use it on your LinkedIn profile. Even if you have only 10 connections, that's okay. It's a start. Don't stress if you feel you lack connections. After speaking to job seekers on a daily basis, I've learned that most people are really not that well connected. Here is your chance to change that right now.

You want to be intentional about the people you connect with. The first step is to start with your own personal network. Pull out your phone and go through your contacts. You will find at least 50–100 people. Connect with them first, and build on that with contacts from Facebook, Instagram, and other social media platforms you're on.

CHAPTER 5

Networking

In Chapter 4, we worked on branding, résumés, LinkedIn, and the job boards. Even after you pass the ATS, it is not enough—that's just the first step. The second step—and the most important one—is networking. When you apply for a job hundreds of other people are applying for, what are the chances of a recruiter or hiring manager randomly picking yours out of those hundreds of other résumés? Slim to none.

According to the top 10 job boards worldwide (Indeed, Monster, Glassdoor, etc.), about 80 percent of jobs are landed through networking. That's why about 80 percent of my time is spent with clients networking and preparing for interviews. Simply submitting job applications is going to get you nowhere.

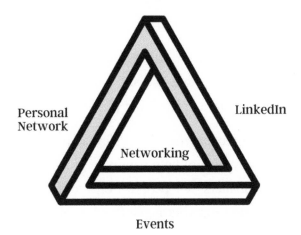

Networking will be split up into three sections: personal network, LinkedIn, and events. We will go through specific details on what to do.

Personal Network

The easiest people to reach out to who might help you in your job search are in your personal network. During years of working in an industry, you are bound to make a few friends and acquaintances. If you scroll through your phone contacts, you will probably find at least 100 numbers. Then you can tap into your social media profiles: Facebook, Instagram, etc.

Start with the first exercise I take my clients through. Take 10 minutes and find 3–5 people from your phone contacts who can help you in your job search. These can be coworkers, friends, neighbors, people with big networks, university friends, family friends, etc. You can include literally anyone you know—don't just think of coworkers, because people know other people. Additionally, having someone refer you to fill an open position at the company they are working for greatly increases your odds. As they say, "It's not what you know, it's who you know."

Start an Excel sheet with different categories and get to work. Every week, keep building that list, and you will start to get creative about what types of people to reach out to.

Send them a simple text message: "Hey, James, I'm looking for a job right now and any type of help would be great. Do you know any recruiters/hiring managers? Or people from your company who can help me? Or someone from your network who can help?"

Work that list and keep track of the dates so you can follow up in the future. Reaching out to these contacts and leveraging your connections can significantly increase your odds of finding a job.

LinkedIn

LinkedIn is probably the most powerful tool in your job-hunting arsenal. The majority (87 percent) of recruiters and hiring managers use LinkedIn to find job candidates. Having a complete profile and being active on your account will garner a lot of attention from recruiters who are seeking professionals to fill positions at their companies. Thus, being active on LinkedIn and making your profile visible to recruiters and companies looking to hire will garner a lot of attention, which translates to messages in your inbox from people looking for someone just like you.

After working with hundreds of clients one-on-one, I've had about 90 percent of them land jobs through LinkedIn. So how do you best leverage LinkedIn for networking?

Step 1

Using the same spreadsheet you used for the personal network, start another sheet so you can keep track of the jobs you are applying for. After applying, put the links into the sheet. In the next column, write down your point of contact for each job. I can tell you the secret sauce of networking in one sentence: have a point of contact for every single job you apply for.

Step 2

Let's say you applied for a position at Google. Go to the LinkedIn search tab and look up (Google) recruiters and then (Google) hiring managers. For each position, connect with at least five to 10 people in that company, and keep track of these connections in your spreadsheet. Higher volume is always better, because some people will respond, while others will not. If people don't respond, don't take it personally. Move on to the next person immediately.

For my clients, I recommend blocking out 45 minutes per day and applying to at least 3–5 jobs (with 5–10 connections for each job). LinkedIn also has an easy-apply option, and you can use filters to specify the location, industry, job level, and more.

All of this adds up to around 50 applications per week and 500 new connections sent out. At the end of the month, you'll have 200 applications and 2,000 connections—it really adds up! It's more about taking small daily actions and making consistent progress versus stressing yourself out and doing it all over the weekend.

LinkedIn is also just like any other social media platform, but the catch is that it is for professionals. You can connect with many like-minded people, grow your network, and get plenty of exposure in your industry. Spending your day connecting with recruiters for companies you are interested in can exponentially boost your chances of finding an opening there.

Many of my clients face the common fear of reaching out to strangers, whether it's an employee at a company or a job recruiter.

Let's shift that idea completely. Number one, the most important thing for you to understand is that a recruiter only get paid their commission when you land the job. Read that again. Recruiters and some hiring managers get paid commissions when applicants sign job offers. When you actively reach out to them, you are doing them a favor and making their lives easier. When you message job recruiters, this means more money in their pockets, which equates to more money to feed their own families.

When I'm working with my clients, we reach out to hundreds and hundreds of people over the course of a few months. Why? Because some people will respond to you, while others will just ignore or reject you. That is normal, and it's part of the game.

If you reach out to someone on LinkedIn and they don't respond to you, it is not even about you, so get rid of that idea completely. I want you to change your mindset into one of a powerful person who will go out there and build genuine relationships with people because you care about them and they care about you! Yes, it's going to be uncomfortable. Yes, you might not feel like it, but that's where the growth is. Push yourself to do it!

Events

Job fairs are an excellent way to grow your personal network. At job fairs, many companies and potential hires are gathered to meet and connect with potential employers and employees. If you are a natural at meeting new people, you might find a large amount of success at a job fair. You are encouraged to leverage your communication skills and sell yourself to these companies. It is a great way to stand out from the crowd and speedrun an interview. Even now, with everything becoming virtual, there are still some Zoom events you can attend. Meetup is one great website for these events, or you can do a simple Google search.

While some may think job fairs are the same as networking events, they are actually very different. The biggest difference is that job fairs are meant for potential candidates to network with companies. However, networking events can be conferences, expositions, and so on, where people from the same industry can attend and network. The goal here is to have your professional business card and some copies of your résumé on hand. This is a great way to meet people in the industry who can help you in your job hunt.

A lot of people have a fear of meeting new people, and going to events might be a challenge. I can tell you so many stories of how random strangers completely changed my life and I literally had nothing to offer them—all I did was simply ask for help. To help you ease your mind, I would like to change your perspective on networking. Asking for help is extremely powerful and far from being a weakness. It shows people you are authentic, which is what people are always looking for.

What is networking? Networking comes down to one simple thing: empathy. Empathy for yourself and empathy for the person in front of you.

Simply make it about building genuine, authentic, and organic relationships. Just like you make friends in the gym. Just like you make friends online on social media. Networking is exactly the same, because whether it's a hiring manager, a VP, or even a CEO, in the end, they are all normal human beings. They have their own insecurities and doubts about themselves. They go through the exact same things every single one of us goes through. If you study the most successful people, you'll find they always give back and help others. They actually enjoy it!

Networking is about getting to know people and caring for them in a nontransactional way, on a personal and organic level. It's as easy as that.

Just ask people: "What do you like? What are your hobbies? What do you find interesting? What are your passions? Tell me about your life." These are the types of simple questions and expressions of interest that start to build genuine relationships.

When building these relationships and asking for help, you can use these guidelines:

- **Ask with confidence and a strong belief in what you're saying.**

  You should be completely convinced about what you are asking.

  Believe from the bottom of your heart that it will work out, no matter what.

- **Create value for the person you're asking.**

  Find one area they need help with and offer to help them with that.

  Even if you help them with something small, that counts.

- **Ask specifically.**

  Define precisely what you need.

  Why do you need it?

  When do you need it?

  What will you produce with it?

- **Ask until you get what you want.**

  Be patient. Some of these people might take some extra time to give you results.

CHAPTER 6

Aligning Body, Mind, and Emotions

We do not always have control over what happens in the outside world, but we can learn to control what happens on the inside.

—Donna Goddard

The Balancing Act: Body

One of the most important keys to success is to be balanced in your life. By balanced, I mean that you take care of all aspects of yourself. Think of your car: when your wheels are out of alignment, it is hard to drive your car effectively. For most people, there is one weakness in their lives that needs more attention so they can be rightly aligned for success.

Though it's obvious, unfortunately, many professionals don't see a direct correlation between fitness and workplace performance, or the thought of a fitness regimen might seem overwhelming. When I talk to job seekers, I always ask them, "How's your health and fitness?" About 70 percent say, "Not so good."

No matter how hard you work and how much money you make, if you sacrifice your physical health, all your work will be futile, and all your money will be useless. Physical health requires balance. Your body was not meant to sit in a chair for eight hours while you load it up with sugar and caffeine. Yet coffee, sweets, and other snack foods are readily available in the office. What office does not have a coffee maker and a vending machine filled with mostly unhealthy snacks?

You don't need to be an athlete to be in good shape. There are three simple steps any business professional can incorporate into their lifestyle. After participating in more than 15 fitness competitions, I've learned a lot of simple yet extremely effective exercise, nutrition, and mindfulness techniques you can incorporate in your own daily life.

Nutrition

Eating the right foods can drastically boost energy levels throughout the day, especially for professionals and businesspeople who usually have hectic days and lots of things on their to-do lists. If you eat too much sugar, your energy levels will drop. If you have a craving for sugar, fruit is the best choice. Eating healthy helps maximize your productivity so you can operate more efficiently and go home at night with some energy left over for your family.

According to research conducted by the Centers for Disease Control and Prevention, the effects of obesity and poor health cost US companies more than $200 billion each year due to lost productivity. Yet most corporate wellness initiatives are superficial and ineffective. In most cases, education around healthy eating does not change eating habits. The key is offering healthy food for free. A growing trend over the last couple of decades is to provide healthy food and snacks at the workplace (at least in the larger tech companies). For instance, Google offers their employees more than 30 different food choices. Facebook has meatless Mondays and a plant-based café at their New York office.

Exercise

In addition to eating well, it is extremely important to have an exercise routine. Sitting for hours on end can increase the risk of chronic health issues such as heart disease. The first step to moving your body is to avoid sitting for long periods of time. Many people spend an hour or more sitting in a car during their daily commute only to sit for eight hours behind a desk. Many will even eat lunch sitting in front of a computer. This is an extremely unhealthy routine. If this resonates with you, you need to get up and move around all day.

Stretching is equally important. After you've been sitting for a while, it is vital to get up and stretch. Some companies, such as Apple and HBO, offer yoga classes for their employees because it is centered around breathing. In yoga, you breathe into your stretches to increase your energy. The more flexible your body is, the more flexible your mind can be. One of the best ways to get an instant charge is to go outdoors if possible. Take your shoes off, ground yourself to the earth, and do some stretching and deep breathing. This will really recharge your battery.

What kind of sports or activities do you like? Whether it's walking, running, lifting weights, hiking, exercising at home, yoga, etc., all you need is 30 minutes of that in your day.

Mornings are the optimal time to exercise because it will boost your metabolism and help you feel energized throughout the whole day.

Not enough time? Simple exercises you can do in the office include:

- Walking up and down the stairs for five to 10 minutes
- Going for a walk around your office building

- Doing arm stretches

- Performing wall or desk push-ups

The key to making this work is consistency. If you exercise three days per week, eat healthy 60 percent to 80 percent of the time, and do the daily mental work, you will start to lose weight and feel more energized, and your professional performance will skyrocket.

We are all human, and we slack sometimes. That's okay. Don't be too hard on yourself. Big improvements start with small steps like these.

Mindfulness

One of the greatest challenges any business will face is the avalanche of stress that can burn out their workforce. Business leaders are held accountable for increased productivity to boost profits, but often, unrealistic expectations can leave workers with chronic levels of stress. Corporate wellness programs have discovered one of the most effective approaches to stress management is mindfulness training.

So what the heck is mindfulness? Mindfulness is a Western adaptation of Eastern meditation and self-awareness processes that have been reinvented to address the lightning-fast speed of our digital workplace.

The core of mindfulness training is becoming more of an observer of your present thoughts and sensations without the need to react or judge. This helps you reduce stress and anxiety and increase resilience. This awareness will certainly improve communication dynamics among coworkers. It will also create an inner quiet that will increase productivity as workers are more focused, open-minded, and aware of the energy around them.

Many companies around the globe have integrated mindfulness training into their workforces, including Goldman Sachs, Intel, Royal Dutch Shell, SAP, and Target. The results are very clear: reduced stress and happier employees. Some companies like Zappos have mindful meditation practices with their teams at the start of the day. Decades ago, no one would have imagined meditation as part of the corporate culture in Western corporations, but in fact, many business leaders practice meditation themselves, such as Salesforce CEO Marc Benioff, Twitter CEO Jack Dorsey, and Google cofounder Sergey Brin. Google has even created silent lunchrooms where you can go to chill out and readjust your mind without having to speak to anyone else.

How can you implement some mindfulness techniques into your workday? The best time to practice mindfulness is when you first wake up. Three great ways to achieve a mindful state are:

- Meditation
- Journaling
- Reading or listening to something positive

Before starting your day, sit in a meditative state for 5 to 10 minutes to set the tone for the day. You can use simple breathing techniques while practicing gratitude, or you can use a meditation app. There are many ways to meditate. YouTube has hundreds of free meditation videos. When you meditate, you slow your brain waves down to the alpha state, which is similar to a trance state in which you are calm enough to receive inspiration from within. This state of consciousness is both relaxed and receptive, and you'll have expanded awareness and openness to receiving new information.

The way we spend this time is pivotal if we want to maximize our performance at work and in business. Just take it from Oprah Winfrey, who meditates every morning. Fill your mind with peaceful and harmonious thoughts as you meditate for five to 15 minutes. After that, journal for five minutes (What are my thoughts for today? What am I grateful for? What are my top goals for the day?) Finally, listen to something positive on your commute to work. These simple techniques are so easy and effective that it won't take long for you to notice how much more productive your days become.

The Power of Visualization

When you think of a big goal or dream you want to achieve, it's natural to think of all the obstacles that might come your way. The problem is that far too often, we allow these obstacles to grow so big in our minds that they keep us from moving forward. Visualization is the number one tool to boost your confidence. It will allow you to push through and overcome these obstacles.

All top performers, regardless of profession, know the importance of picturing themselves succeeding. Visualizing yourself succeeding at a goal before it happens will boost your confidence and your belief system, and it will enhance your abilities, habits, and attitudes.

The brain can't distinguish between imagination and reality, so when you feed your mind the idea of succeeding, it activates something called the RAS (Reticular Activating System). This is the part of your brain that moves ideas from the conscious mind to the subconscious mind.

When I first started my journey here in the United States, the only thing I had was my vision of working at Qualcomm. I had no job, no experience, and no friends or family nearby. I was building a brand-new life. I thought about that vision every single day, and it kept me going when challenges arose. Doing this doesn't guarantee you will see your vision come to life, but it will strengthen your faith. When you truly let go of the need to control circumstances, you will discover greater ease in accomplishing the things you really want.

Visualization has scientifically proven benefits:

- Improves performance

- Helps you reach your potential

- Reduces stress

- Sparks inspiration

- Boosts confidence and creativity

- Can make you feel better and heal faster if you are sick and visualize good health

- Helps you overcome nervousness

Visualizing Your Dream Job

Now that you know what you want, you have the power to hold a vision of receiving the most fulfilling job offer for you.

For example, say you know your dream job would be in software engineering at a specific company. You know what your dream salary would be, and you know the job would include stock options, insurance, and benefits. If you get a nice top-level office with an ocean view, that would be sweet, too!

Step One

Make sure you have a quiet space where you will not be distracted by noise. (Keep your electronic devices turned off).

Step Two

In order to slow your mind down and get into a relaxed state, inhale deeply through your nose, hold for a count of five, exhale through your mouth, and count to five.

Step Three

Once you are relaxed, close your eyes and start imagining yourself contacting recruiters. Feel what it is like to be confident and comfortable. Now imagine getting the job offer. See and feel yourself sitting in an office with a view. Feel the excitement in your body. Make the vision very clear. Feel the emotions as if your vision is 100 percent real and successful. Take five minutes every day and put your thoughts and emotions into this vision. You can include it as part of your meditation in the morning.

Emotional Intelligence

We are all familiar with the term intelligence quotient (IQ), but for many, the term EQ (which describes emotional intelligence) is an enigma. Simply, EQ is having the ability to recognize your feelings and to manage and express them in a healthy, positive way. It also involves the skill of being an empathetic listener when others are expressing their feelings. This skill is critical for anyone who is a leader or manager.

Our emotions are an integral part of our humanity. Feeling is one of the basic functions of being alive. Your dog or cat may not be able to study for the bar exam, but it can certainly feel and express sadness, anger, and joy. But many of us grow up basically illiterate about our emotions. Boys are told to be tough and that being emotional is a sign of weakness. Girls are ridiculed as being drama queens when they express their emotions. In grade school, no one teaches us about the ABCs of feelings.

Yet in the world of corporate training, emotional intelligence has gained much traction. As more and more leaders and human resources directors are trained in emotional intelligence, they will be able to identify and seek out new employees who have high EQs. They understand a candidate with a higher level of emotional intelligence will be better at collaboration and teamwork. That is because being an active listener and clearly communicating ideas means a person will work with others more effectively.

In addition, the emotionally intelligent candidate will most likely have a more positive outlook and be more resilient, motivated, and productive. Being emotionally intelligent does not mean being overly emotional but rather balanced between thinking and feeling.

While emotions should not be the primary driver when making business decisions and managing others, being more self-aware can certainly help you navigate emotions (and relationships) in a more effective way. In most leadership and management positions, relationship management is a necessary skill.

The Emotionally Intelligent Workplace

A workplace with emotionally intelligent people will be a more joyful workplace. This is because there is mutual respect and compassion that comes with being more emotionally fluid. Training people to be more empathetic, active listeners will reduce workplace conflict. When communication is poor and people harbor bad feelings toward others, it degrades the morale of the team. At times, this can result in increased stress, sickness, and loss of productivity.

Increasing Your EQ

Honor Your Feelings

Do not suppress your feelings. Instead, pause, take a breath, and recognize what you are feeling.

All of us experience many different emotions throughout the day, both negative and positive. The most common negative ones are fear, stress, anger, and anxiety. No matter how grounded you are, you are still going to experience these emotions.

For example: if you keep thinking over and over, *I won't be able to finish this work on time*, your brain signals this thought to your nervous system, and you start to feel it in your body (muscle tightness, shoulders slouched, etc.). If you keep focusing more and more attention on it, it gets worse and worse, so it becomes anxiety.

How do you deal with this? I learned a simple trick from the Iceman himself, Wim Hof, the man who climbed parts of Mount Everest wearing nothing but shorts and shoes. He discovered breathing was the most powerful way to control the mind. That is what allowed him to survive extreme low temperatures.

When you start to feel anxious or stressed, pause. Stop everything you are doing and breathe for two full minutes. Take deep, long breaths. Inhale through the nose and slowly exhale through the mouth. Studies have shown that two minutes of deep breathing decreases your heart rate. Hence, you calm down.

After the two minutes of breathing, put your hands over your heart. Focus on your heartbeat. For one full minute, think about what you are grateful for in your life. Gratitude is the strongest emotion you can call upon to beat all the negative ones. Within those three minutes, you can completely calm yourself down and get back to normal.

If you want to take it a step further and master your emotions, after those three minutes, pick up your phone or a notepad and write down your thoughts for two more minutes. When you put your thoughts on paper, it will release the noise in your mind and relax you even more. Think of it as taking out the trash. When you write down your thoughts and realize how much of them are nonsense, it will make you feel much better about yourself and shift your mind toward more positive ideas.

Don't Be a Hot Reactor

If someone pushes your buttons and you want to fire back, pause, take a breath, and respond from a balanced place.

Think about how bullies operate. A bully says or does certain things to trigger another person to get a reaction. If they get the reaction, they feel satisfied. So basically, if you give in to what they are saying, that's how you lose.

The best way to deal with that is remarkably simple but requires a lot of patience and practice. Basically, it's the good old-fashioned reverse psychology trick. If someone gets angry at you, your natural response is to get angry and fight back, which will escalate the situation and make it worse. Instead, try this: if someone gets angry at you and starts shouting, pause, take a deep breath, look at them, and simply smile. If they keep screaming, do not say anything, and keep smiling. The person will think you are crazy, but what you are doing is breaking their pattern, and that is how you win. Eventually, they will calm down. Only at that point will you be able to resolve your differences.

If you study Buddhism, you know one of its teachings instructs us to be in response mode versus being in reactive mode. What does that mean? Let's say, for example, you wake up in the morning and as you get out of bed, you spill water all over your clothes. In reactive mode, you get angry, agitated, and hate yourself, but in response mode, you laugh and carry on with your day. There is so much power in this. Imagine letting go of all the small things you allow to mess up your day: traffic, accidents, forgetting things, losing things, etc. Consider how much energy you waste by being reactive to these trivial things. Wouldn't it be a relief to let them go? Small changes = big life improvements.

Empower Others

Focus on the good in others and let them know how you feel. This will help you cultivate a greater sense of appreciation.

Whatever religion you practice or do not practice, you have heard of the concept of "karma," which simply means that if you do good things, you get good things, and vice versa. There are so many bad things going on in the world: wars, disease, starvation, politics, and the list goes on and on. You turn on the news and hear nothing but horrible things that make you scared to fall asleep at night.

It is quite simple: if you focus your attention and energy on these bad things, you will see and get more bad things, but if you disregard the negatives and focus on better things that will positively impact you, you will get better and better things.

It's the same when it comes to people. You can focus on their good qualities or their bad qualities. Everyone has good qualities, even the people you dislike. Leadership is all about empowering others and finding their good qualities. Whenever you have a chance to make someone feel good, just do it. It will come back to you in a multitude of other ways.

One particular story I heard completely changed my perspective about being kind to others. There was a guy back in the '70s who wanted to make a name for himself by shooting the president (this is a true story, and the guy wrote a book about it). He hid a gun in his backpack and went to a rally where the president was giving a speech. After waiting for hours, he finally found the right spot where he could accurately aim and shoot from.

As he was walking to get into position, he accidently bumped into an older lady. She turned to him with a smile, apologized, and hugged him to make sure he was okay. The guy completely froze, and his heart was filled with joy. The lady smiled again, waved goodbye, and left.

The guy was so touched by her that he couldn't reach for his gun. He stood there for half an hour trying to do it, but he couldn't, all because of that one random act of kindness from a stranger! After that, he left and went home. So you see, one word or act can save lives.

Listen to and Feel Others

By being an active listener without the constant need to add your two cents, you let other people know you care about what they think. This will help you cultivate a greater sense of empathy.

My father was my biggest idol, and he recently passed away at the age of 88. He truly lived a long and beautiful life. Nine kids, 20 grandkids, and five great-grandkids are his legacy. He has a very powerful story.

My father was born in 1929. He grew up in the post-World War I economic recession and lived through the nightmare of World War II. He was the oldest in a family of five brothers and five sisters. He came from nothing. When he was eight years old, my grandfather let him work, and when my grandfather became ill, my father became the man of the house. When he came of age, he got a business education, learned English, and got a job in accounting, which was very prestigious at that time. Eventually, he built a company and became one of the top businessmen in Jordan.

His life was an interesting one. He traveled the world and knew so many people. A great quality my dad had was to live simply and be empathetic toward others while remaining humble. He taught us these same values.

At his funeral, hundreds of people I had never seen in my life showed up. We are a huge family alone, but the number of people who showed up was amazing. I talked to many of them and asked, "What will you mostly remember about my father?"

Despite his professional success, almost none of them even talked about that. I heard answers like "He helped me build my house when I was poor," "He was kind to me," and "His smile made my day." Friends and family would talk on and on about how kind and empathetic he was, and that is why they loved him. As Maya Angelou said, "I've learned that people will forget what you said, people will forget what you did, but people will never forget how you made them feel."

I am a big believer in that, and my father was the perfect example. Empathy is the most important quality you absolutely need to carry in your personal and professional life. That is what leadership is all about.

CHAPTER 7

The Job Search Success Mindset

Success is not final, failure is not fatal: it is the courage to continue that counts.

—Winston S. Churchill

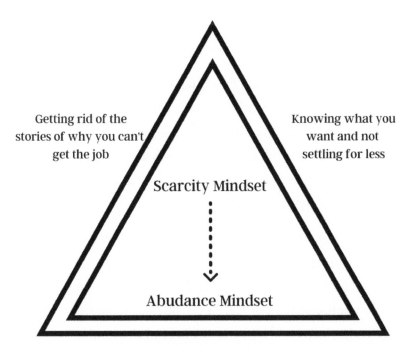

Getting rid of the stories of why you can't get the job

Knowing what you want and not settling for less

Scarcity Mindset

Abudance Mindset

Understanding how to deal with rejection& failure

Building Your Confidence and Embracing Optimism

How is it that we lose confidence over time? When we were children, we felt we could do anything. We had no self-critic when we made drawings in kindergarten. Then we began to compare ourselves to others or endure criticism from others and established a self-image from the programming of other people's judgements of ourselves. Eventually our self-esteem begins to reflect how we think others see us.

If you are in a job interview, an astute interviewer can read your body language and assess your self-confidence. In many cases, we lose confidence because we feel unworthy. Someone who has been rejected after many job interviews can adopt a mindset of expecting rejection. Mindset directs your self-dialogue and becomes a lens through which you view reality. If you have a mindset that expects rejection, you will be less successful than someone who's optimistic and expects to rise.

Being an optimist is about expecting positive outcomes. Optimists are generally hopeful and instilled with a sense of confidence in many areas of life. How can you develop an optimistic mindset? It is like changing a lens—it's all about perspective. View hardships as learning experiences. Consider temporary setbacks as challenges for you to soldier on through until you succeed.

I worked with a fellow named Charles. Charles was a perfectionist, but he was also very pessimistic. He set a very high bar for himself. Charles was a brilliant engineer with a stellar résumé, but he was just not getting traction in his job interviews. My suspicion was that Charles did not exude excitement because his overall disposition was a bit of a drag. I sat Charles down and discovered he had a self-sabotaging pattern of feeling anxious that he could not deliver on the expectations of the jobs he was applying for. He could not get excited by any new challenges because of his fear of failure.

Sometimes you have to say yes with excitement, trust you will learn what you need on the job, and know that you can reach out for support. Charles was the kind of person who would not reach out for support and would try to figure it out on his own.

Someone like Charles is fearful of being vulnerable. Being vulnerable does not mean you are weak. It means you are humble enough to ask for support in life. In the current business climate, coaching is essential in most sectors. Charles eventually found a great coach to help him work on his interviewing skills and is now happily employed.

As you integrate the tools and approaches defined in this book, you will gain the confidence to ace any interview. By embodying the higher principles of your personal vision, your branding strategy will feel very organic and authentic. The key is to cultivate a powerful belief in yourself to maneuver the many obstacles you could face. Be certain of your value.

Why do we lose confidence? The first time I meet any potential client, I start with two main questions: 1) What are your problems and biggest challenges? 2) What do you need help with the most? After talking on the phone with thousands of people, I've learned everyone has one common problem: *rejection*. Do any of these sound familiar?

- "I applied online hundreds of times and got ghosted."

- "I had five interviews and got rejected."

- "Hiring managers are rejecting me left and right."

- "I networked and heard nothing back."

All of this piles on to the stress that comes from family obligations, bills, and more. This is why we start to lose confidence in ourselves and make things personal. We think things like:

- "I'm not good enough for the job."

- "I don't have the skills."

- "There are no jobs."

- "The economy is bad."

- "I'm too old/too young."

We keep telling ourselves these stories over and over until eventually, we believe them. This creates something I like to call the **"scarcity mindset."** Going into an interview with this mindset is setting yourself up for failure. You are operating from a needy place, a place of desperation to get the job or pay the bills. Think about dating. If you show up to a date *desperate* for attention or validation from that person, they will run away like the wind!

When you're talking to an interviewer, hiring manager, or recruiter, they will feel this type of needy energy, which will completely turn them off, and they will move on to the next person ASAP.

How do you move away from the scarcity mindset to the other side, which is the **"abundance mindset"**? Let's define it. An abundance mindset is when you put yourself in a position of power. Not a dictator's type of power, but your true power. This comes down to three main points:

1. Getting rid of stories about why you can't get the job

2. Knowing what you want and not settling for less

3. Understanding how to deal with rejection and building confidence

1. Getting Rid of the Stories about Why You Can't Get the Job

The first step is to get rid of all your negative beliefs, which are the mental blocks that we all have. These are the stories we have in our minds about why we can't get the job.

For example:

- "I'm too old."

- "I'm too young."

- "I'm an introvert."

- "People don't like me."

- "The economy sucks."

- "There are no jobs in my city."

- "I don't believe in myself or my abilities."

- "Maybe they won't like me."

These are the types of stories that are holding us back from many, many things. Right now, as you're reading this, ask yourself, "What is the story I keep telling myself over and over about the job search?" Jot all these stories down. Awareness is the first step toward building the abundance mindset.

The second step is to flip the script. Whatever negative stories you wrote down on the paper, flip them into positive ones. For example, "I'm too old" becomes "I have a lot of experience to offer." If you feel too young, then try "I have a lot of new perspectives, innovation, and new ideas to introduce to the company."

Write down whatever resonates with you the most. Read these new stories on this sheet of paper out loud every single morning to engrave them in your mind. This will take time because you have been telling yourself the old stories for such a long time that they are stuck in your head. As the weeks pass, however, these old stories will fade away and the new stories will start to kick in.

Going into an interview with these new stories in mind will allow you to be more confident and have a strong tone of voice. Only 7 percent of communication is the actual words you speak, and the rest is body language and tonality, so tonality alone is very powerful.

Let me tell you the story of one of my clients, Joe. When I first met Joe, he was deeply steeped in the scarcity mindset. He had recently applied to numerous jobs, talked to recruiters, and even gone through many interviews, but none of them had transformed into anything— nothing, no offers.

He was also under a lot of financial stress from his wife and faced tremendous pressure to pay a growing stack of bills. This went on for more than eight months. He continued to tell himself he was a failure who could not provide for his family. Furthermore, his wife had been laid off, amplifying his own sense of desperation and anxiety.

This desperation seeped through in every interview. His disposition was needy, and his confidence was lacking. This lack of confidence can easily derail an interview. The interviewer, not knowing your personal history or current adversities, will often mistake your desperation for inability.

I worked with him for two weeks, and we got rid of all his negative stories. We talked about his debt as a challenge he could overcome, not a reflection of his failures. He started to focus on all his strengths:

his experience, his charisma, and his leadership and technical skills. Shortly after that, he landed a $150,000 offer at his dream company. We didn't even do any of the technical work, such as revising his résumé or prepping for interviews. What he did was a shift from the scarcity mindset to the abundance mindset. I'm not saying that mindset alone will get you the job, but it is a huge factor that will affect your success in your job search.

Alina, on the other hand, had a good mindset, but she still wasn't tapping 100 percent into her true abundant mindset. She has a fascinating personal history, including being one of the first-star snowboarders featured in one of the first sports documentaries in Russia.

Yet her old stories continued to tell her she was not worthy of a higher salary. I worked with her, and within a couple of weeks, she had landed an offer that was 20 percent higher than her current salary. This happened when she flipped the script. Her mindset changed from "I don't have enough experience to receive x salary" to "While I may have fewer years on the job, my fresh perspective and positive energy alongside my existing rich experience make me an ideal candidate."

Years ago, I met Eric, a senior professional with more than a decade of experience in sales. He has an incredible background that includes working at some of the top global tech companies. Unfortunately, Eric had been laid off due to a company acquisition, which took a significant toll on his confidence and self-worth. To make matters worse, a close family member was dealing with significant health issues. Needless to say, his life was seeming to fall apart at his feet. His situation was more severe than the scarcity mindset discussed at the beginning of this chapter.

He was applying to jobs, and nothing worked—failed interviews, rejection, you name it. I knew how much talent he had, and nothing was wrong with his background. His biggest problem was the mental state he was in.

The concept of shifting his mindset was foreign to him, and he had zero interest in changing it. The first time we spoke on the phone, we had a long two-hour conversation. I was trying to help him and bring him in as a client. That also didn't work out.

Many months later, we reconnected on LinkedIn, and he was still looking for a job. I told him, "Completely forget about the job. Let me just help you get back on track mentally, with no obligations whatsoever." He finally agreed.

Weeks later, he started to feel a hint of optimism amidst all the challenges he faced. I taught him to start meditating so he could calm his mind and better deal with adversity. Additionally, we worked on building strong habits of mind and getting rid of the false narratives he was telling himself. We worked on deconstructing his negative self-talk and catastrophizing tendencies. Believe it or not, as stubborn as he was, he did it.

He noticed the mental shifts, and he liked them. We developed a very strong friendship throughout this process. His business mentality blew my mind, and his ideas were very innovative. Through our conversations I learned a lot from him in many different areas, including leadership, sales, and operations. He is a human encyclopedia of information. He also has a big heart and truly cares about helping others, and we share a lot of values. One day, it just hit me: "Forget about working at other companies. Let's work together!" I saw how much talent he had and truly believed with all my heart that he would thrive if given the right opportunity.

Boom! We started working together, and it was a great fit! We both continuously grow from working together, and he has helped me grow personally and professionally.

2. Knowing What You Want and Not Settling for Less

When you don't know what you want, you can easily settle for anything. Most people take random jobs they hate just to pay the bills. That is a trap. I've worked with clients who make $350K per year and are miserable. They make all that money, but they come back home to their families and let out all the stress and frustration on them, which results in more unhappiness.

Take a stand and stick to what makes you happy. When you go into an interview and know what you want, that is a complete game changer. You will show them they need you and you don't need them. That is what being in a position of power is all about. I will dive more deeply into how to define your dream job and know what you want in the following chapters.

3. Understanding How to Deal with Rejection and Building Confidence

Rejection is hard. Some adults have not healed from childhood rejection. The perfectionist may have developed their pessimistic mindset early in their childhood, perhaps because of strict and demanding parents. If a person never felt like they were good enough as a child, whether it was getting good grades or performing well at sports, they can carry that self-judgement around and project that demeanor during an interview. They might even subconsciously sabotage an interview by saying something that may sound insecure. This is because they might have a hard time building trust. Building trust creates rapport.

However, rejection is a natural part of life. In a way, it is a sign you are taking risks and living a more fearless life. If you never get rejected, it may be because you are fearful of exploring outside your comfort zone. When it comes to taking risks and applying for jobs, you may feel the positions are out of your league, which is completely normal: nearly every single person I talk to deals with what's called "imposter syndrome."

When you develop an attitude of self-confidence and passion, a keen interviewer can feel your energy, and you will make an impression. Sometimes the interviewer will be so impressed with your presence they will find you are worth investing in.

If rejection is an issue for you, here are some steps you can take to work through the emotional resistance. Most importantly, give yourself permission to feel your emotions. If you feel anger or sadness, don't suppress it. Don't lie to yourself or others about how you are feeling. A response like "no big deal" when you're crushed inside does not work. You may end up projecting the anger harboring inside you at another person for no reason.

Instead of letting rejection bring you down, let it power you up. Spend time with people who empower you and reinforce your awesomeness. Take time each day to appreciate what you have created in your life so far and focus on what you want for your future. If you can hold that future vision of your ultimate success and feel worthy of reaching the height of success, 50 percent of the work is done. The other 50 percent of the work is to reverse engineer the milestones you've achieved on the way to your ultimate success.

Understand that everyone goes through these things, from junior professionals all the way up to directors and CEOs. It is inevitable, and it is part of the game, not just in the job search.

Consider any goal you would like to accomplish. You will face some kind of rejection or failure. When you were a baby, you fell many times until you learned how to walk. If you are an athlete, you're not going to get the gold medal in the Olympics on the first try. You have to go through many failures. While you're going after your goals, things will not always move in the way you think they're supposed to, because that is life. You will get hit with different things. The biggest differentiator between successful and unsuccessful people is how they deal with rejection and failure.

Most of us deal with rejection by feeling anger, frustration, doubt, and blame and losing faith and confidence in ourselves. These emotions rinse and repeat, and over time, this gets worse and worse as they stack on top of each other.

To flip this script, you need to change your perspective about rejection. Understand that it is a numbers game. If you connect with 10 recruiters, about half will respond to your request. Out of those five, only one or two will have a phone conversation with you. When someone ghosts you, move on to the next person, fast! Understand these recruiters get bombarded with messages, and sometimes they simply forget to message you back.

The most important thing for mentally dealing with rejection is this: don't take it personally. Don't make it about you, because that contributes to the scarcity mindset. See yourself as playing a basketball game. Out of a hundred free throws, at least 50 will go in. Just keep pushing forward, and don't focus on the 50 missed shots.

CHAPTER 8

The Confidence Triad

Believe in your infinite potential. Your only limitations are those you set upon yourself.

—Roy T. Bennett

Getting Rid of Negative
Beliefs/Stories

Dealing with
Failure/Rejection

Mental Fitness

In previous chapters, we talked about the first two pillars of the Confidence Triad: 1) getting rid of old stories and 2) how to deal with failure and rejection. Now let's get into the third pillar: mental fitness. When you go to the gym, you need to train consistently. Over time, your muscles will grow and get stronger. The mind is the same. Mental fitness is built through mental exercises. The more you do them, the more your mental muscle will get stronger.

On average, we have 60,000 thoughts per day, and research shows 80 percent of these thoughts are useless. This includes thoughts that cause stress, doubt, fear, anxiety, and joy as well as a big mix of negative and positive stories. By doing mental exercises, you'll feed your mind more positive things that will override the negatives. This helps to build the abundance mindset that we talked about in the previous chapter. Obviously, this is not some type of magic that will work overnight; it takes time and consistency. As the months go by, you will get stronger and stronger.

Just as with any other new habit, when you start, it's natural for your mind to push back with thoughts like "Hey, don't do this. It is silly and it will never work." "I am tired. I'll do it tomorrow." "I don't have time," and more. Just keep at it. The results will surprise you. Mental fitness simply means having a daily regimen or habit that helps you prime your mind to have a successful day. This is the most significant step that will move you from the scarcity mindset into abundance.

Almost all successful people have daily morning rituals or habits that help them get going. You can't wake up and just hope you'll be in a good mood for the day. You have to demand that your brain and body put you in the best state of mind, one that will set you up for success throughout the whole day.

I've adapted the techniques of Tony Robbins, Tim Ferriss, and others and created my own simple daily routine that really puts me in the zone. Do this as soon as you wake up, because that's the way to get the best results!

Step 1: Make your Bed (1–3 mins.)

This is the first and easiest success of your day. Giving your brain this small dose of success will trigger it for even more success throughout the day.

Step 2: Exercise (15–30 mins.)

This can be walking, jogging, home exercises, or playing sports—any form of movement that gets the blood flowing.

Scientifically proven benefits of physical activity:

- Controls weight

- Reduces risk of cardiovascular disease, type 2 diabetes, metabolic syndrome, cancers

- Strengthens bones and muscles

- Improves mental health and mood

- Improves your ability to do daily activities

- Increases your chances of living longer

Step 3: Meditation (10 mins.)

- Breath exercise (1 min.): Hands up, breathe in through nose; hands down, breath out through nose. Do three sets of 30 reps each.

- With your eyes closed, your body relaxed, and headphones playing relaxing music:

- Gratitude (3 mins.): Think of three to five things you are grateful for in your life. Live in that moment; appreciate these things and be thankful that you have them.

- Blessings (3 mins.): Think of all the people you love and who love you back. Send them blessings and good vibes to make their day better and help them with whatever struggles they are going through.

- Visualization (3 mins.): Think of the top three goals you want to accomplish during the day. Go through the process of successfully completing each task and celebrating victory.

Scientifically proven benefits of meditation:

- Reduces stress

- Improves concentration

- Encourages a healthy lifestyle

- Increases self-awareness, happiness, and acceptance

- Slows aging

- Benefits cardiovascular and immune health

Step 4: The 5-Minute Journal (5 mins.)

Complete these three sections in your journal each morning:

- What are three things you are grateful for?

- What are three things you want to accomplish today?

- Write down three affirmations.

Two questions to answer every night:

- What are three amazing things that happened today?

- How could I have made today even better?

Scientifically proven benefits of gratitude:

- Opens the door to more relationships

- Improves physical and psychological health

- Enhances empathy and reduces aggression

- Promotes better sleep and self-esteem

- Increases mental strength

Step 5: Read or Listen to Inspirational Material for 15–30 minutes

You can incorporate this into your workout so it won't take extra time.

Top motivational speakers I like: Tony Robbins, Les Brown, Eric Thomas, Gary Vaynerchuck (hundreds of videos are available on YouTube, such as this one: https://www.youtube.com/watch?v=hBP-YBX597s&t=477s).

Scientifically proven benefits of listening to or reading inspirational material:

- Relieves stress and anxiety

- Improves cognitive abilities

- Increases concentration

- Pumps you up

- Increases focus

- Drowns out negativity and uncertainty

CHAPTER 9

How to Nail Interviews

A lot of us, for instance, are very good at our jobs but are absolutely hopeless at job interviews.

—Karl Wiggins

Now we are going to get into the exact details of how to prepare for the interview, from logistics to interview questions and, finally, negotiating the salary.

1. Relating your experience to the job description

Let's start with relating your experience to the job. The job description will be your secret weapon when you're applying for any type of job. It is the company's love language. Think about it this way: when hiring managers are talking to different candidates, they have the job descriptions right in front of them. They are comparing everything you say, point by point, with what they're looking for. So you have to understand that every single answer you provide should be relatable to the job description.

For example, if the first part of the job is Python programming, go back to your résumé and dig into all your projects, coursework, jobs, freelance work, skills—every single thing in your life that is related to Python programming. Even if you have very little experience with it, it is worth mentioning that you took a course on Python.

A second example would be leadership. If the job description states something about leading teams, think about what kinds of teams you worked with in the past (engineering, sales, marketing, etc.). Even go back to your college days: What type of courses or programs did you take?

Let's use this sample job description. Under each point, using your résumé, write down some summarized bullets:

Key Responsibilities:

1. **Collaborate with engineering teams to support the full life cycle of flight electronics, design analysis**

   - Worked with engineering teams for 8 years (Google, Amazon, MBA program)

2. **Interface with vendors as the technical representative and subcontractors manager**

   - 2 years working with vendors

   - Worked as a subcontractor for multiple projects

3. **Perform electronic design**

   - 2 years of design using AutoCAD, PLS-CADD

Basic Qualifications:

1. **5+ years of experience developing high-reliability electronics or embedded systems**

   - 3 years at Qualcomm, 5 years at Rite Aid

   - 2 certifications

2. **Extensive experience in design and programming**

   - 10 years of design, 7 years of programming (C++, Python, SQL, MATLAB)

3. **Practical experience with PCB assembly and design**

   - 3 years

Desired Qualifications:

1. **Master's degree in electrical engineering**

2. **Experience in developing C/C++**

3. **Experience developing firmware for embedded systems**

   - 2 years, multiple projects, start-up, extra courses, programs

Commonality points with the interviewer/interviewers

In the job description or email invite, they always mention the person or people you will be interviewing with. It is very powerful when you go in with some commonality points so you can break the ice and build a genuine relationship with them.

Most people think the interviewer is some evil person who is trying to make you fail. Whether it's a director or manager, they are simply human beings with doubts, fears, and insecurities, just like all of us. If you are thinking, *I hope I don't mess this up*, they are thinking, *Oh, I really hope I ask the right type of questions and don't look stupid.* So relax and think of this person as your friend.

To find out some commonality points, go to their LinkedIn profile. Most professionals are on there, but if the interviewer isn't, do a Google search for their name to find other social media profiles. Commonality topics can be sports, common connections, education, companies they worked for, their hometown, or shared interests.

Studying the company

You need to go in with a good idea about the company and if it is aligned with your own values and goals. Here's what you'll find to find out:

1) Overview and summary

2) Short-term and long-term goals

3) Online reviews

There are a bunch of resources where you can get this information. My favorites are:

www.google.com

www.glassdoor.com

www.vault.com

www.wikipedia.org

Let's say you are interviewing with Google. Under each section, jot down some bullet points that you got from the websites mentioned above.

1) Overview and summary

- Great benefits and work environment

- Rewards good performance

- Member focused

- Good range of products

- Values diversity of employees

2) Short-term and long-term goals

- 30, 60, 90-day plans

- Build good relationships with team members and boss

- Achieve x quotas by the end of the first year

- Promotion within 2 years

3) Online reviews

- Great company culture

- Great benefits

- Work-life balance

- Technology focused

- $88K pay online

2. The interview success mindset

After years of prepping clients for interviews, I've learned and seen common patterns with all types of interviews (junior, mid and senior level). I boiled it down to a mental formula you can use over and over when going into any type of situation.

The first thing I want you to understand is that no one answers all the questions perfectly. It's impossible. After working with hundreds of people, I've learned you are bound to mess up on some of the questions, and that is perfectly okay. Don't think that if you don't answer all the questions, you will lose the job. Relax, be yourself, and put them at ease. Be friendly instead of formal. The more conversational you are, the more the interviewer will like and connect with you.

The second thing I want you to keep in mind is that it's not *what* you answer—it's *how* you answer questions. Effective communication = 7 percent words, 38 percent tone of voice, and 55 percent body language. The words you say have very little impact. In fact, 93 percent of your success in the interview will depend on the other two factors!

This is where mental fitness is valuable. Ultimately, a positive mindset will aid you in developing a strong tone of voice and self-assured body language (93 percent of your performance). When you are more confident, your body language will show it, and your tone of voice will be stronger and more assertive.

A third thing I want you to keep in mind is that no one knows how you actually prepared, which means if you answer a question in a different way than you practiced, that's okay. Just own it. Also, in the interview, it's normal to get nervous, and sometimes you might forget what words to say, but go ahead and speak from the heart. It's never going to be perfect.

Research shows that even if you don't answer the questions 100 percent correctly but your delivery is confident and you show no hesitation, the interviewer will definitely like that, and you'll pass. But if, for example, there is a series of tests (let's say you're applying for an engineering company) you must go through, your studying and preparation will be key and will highly benefit you.

Most interviews are the non-test type, and the process I will show you in this section will arm you with the tools you need to have a great advantage. Always remember how unique and powerful you are and that you have unlimited potential. Going back to the quote I mentioned earlier in the book, "Companies invest in people and not in résumés."

In 1954, scientists around the world agreed that no person could run a mile in less than four minutes. Then came Roger Bannister, who broke that rule and ran a mile in 3:59.4. The point here is that all the scientists in the world can't dictate how much potential and power you have. Don't let anyone or anything make you feel otherwise.

Now, get ready to build a powerful belief system that will help you own *all* the interviews you go to.

For now (for the non-test part of the interview), we will work on having the right psychology that will give you the confidence you need to push through *any question*. Even if you've prepared for a hundred hours, if you don't believe from the bottom of your heart that you'll nail the interview, it won't happen. Having a strong belief system will give you confidence. Even if you don't know the "right" answer to a question, you'll still find a way to answer it.

What are your beliefs about interviewing? Let's dig deep, find those old negative beliefs, and replace them with new empowering ones.

Don't believe the introvert/extrovert garbage. No one should be labeled as any single thing. You are an amazing, unique, and powerful individual.

Step 1: Let's start with your old beliefs. What do you believe you can do with the interview?

Examples of negative beliefs:

- I don't know what to say in the interview.

- I feel overqualified/underqualified.

- What if I don't get the offer?

- I'm an introvert.

- What if I don't answer all the questions?

- The interviewer might not like me.

Step 2: Now it's time to destroy those silly old beliefs and leave them all behind. Instead, let's get you started on building more powerful positive beliefs.

These are examples of some of the beliefs I had about myself when I started to do interviews:

- I will answer all the questions and nail them, no matter what.

- I will nail the interview.

- The interviewer will love me.

- I'll win.

- I'll get the job.

- I am freaking awesome, talented, amazing, and powerful beyond measure. No one and nothing can stop me!

- I have what it takes to win this interview, and I believe that from the bottom of my heart.

- I'm not afraid of failure, rejection, doubt, or anything else. I am a beast.

- I will push through and always win.

These beliefs might sound weird, and you might not believe them now, but what you need to do is read them out loud and write them down in the morning when you wake up as part of your journaling. Remember the daily habits we mentioned in the previous chapter: 1) meditation, 2) journaling, 3) exercise, and 4) feeding your mind something positive.

Every day, as you read, write, and say them out loud, they will be programmed into your conscious and subconscious mind. You'll slowly start to feel your confidence grow. When you go to that interview, you won't even have to think about it. It will be a part of you, and the interviewer will sense that.

Start building the habit of writing down these new beliefs in the morning and reading these phrases out loud throughout the day. Do the same at night before you go to sleep so they can become a part of your conscious and subconscious mind.

I'm not saying negative thoughts, old beliefs, and doubt will never hit you. These things will come, but when you read and write these phrases out loud over and over every day, you will start to phase out the old thoughts, and your brain will start to focus on these new empowering beliefs.

This is not a one-day process. You need to do this every single day for a long period of time because you have years of programming—internalized negative beliefs from your parents, society, TV, and other people—to undo. It's going to take some time to replace them with these new powerful, positive ones.

Let's talk about the actual questions and how to prepare. After working with my clients and doing hundreds of hours of interview preparation, I've learned that there are a lot of generic questions they ask over and over almost every time, and after we discuss the generic questions, we will dive into the company/role-specific types of questions.

Interview Questions

My favorite format to use for answering questions is the STAR method.

S: Situation

T: Task

A: Action

R: Result

If you feel you usually get stuck in giving long or short answers, this will help you a lot. All you need to do is jot down bullet points under each letter for the main ideas you want to communicate. Don't write sentences or long scripts. You will forget those.

Example:

Tell me about a time you handled a difficult client?

S: Client dropped us when I was at Amazon

T: Find out what the problem was, meet with the team, figure out a solution

A: Met with client, found common ground, used the proposed solution with them

R: Client still dropped but gave us a referral

To put all of this together, you want to hit on these main points and speak from the heart. You can use the STAR format for these upcoming generic questions or use the explanations below.

1) The top 10 generic questions

Let's use the same sample job description we used earlier.

Key Responsibilities:

A) **Collaborate with engineering teams to support the full life cycle of flight electronics, design analysis**

B) **Interface with vendors as the technical representative and subcontractors manager**

C) **Perform electronic design**

Basic Qualifications:

A) **5+ years of experience developing high-reliability electronics or embedded systems**

B) **Extensive experience in design and programming**

C) **Practical experience with PCB assembly and design**

Desired Qualifications:

A) **Master's degree in electrical engineering**

B) **Experience in developing C/C++**

C) **Experience developing firmware for embedded systems**

Question 1: What is your greatest strength?

Two things to keep in mind here: your tangible and nontangible strengths.

Nontangible: Good leader, manager, loves customers, empathetic, etc.

Tangible: Go back to the job description and talk about the things you are strongest in (programming, working with engineering teams, C++, etc.)

Question 2: What is your greatest weakness?

Talk about your weaknesses in the areas that are not included in the job description or something you struggled with in the past. Then mention that you worked on improving and add a positive aspect to it by focusing on the solution you came up with. Be honest. It shows confidence (nobody's perfect).

Example:

- I wasn't organized when I was growing up, but I learned a time management system.

- Sometimes I multitask too much, so I lose track of time.

- I tend to procrastinate on some projects, but I always get my work done before the deadline. I learned to start working on projects a week early.

Question 3: Tell me about yourself.

Here you literally have to be yourself and talk to the interviewer as if they were your childhood friend. Talk about your hobbies and passions (surfing, skiing, fitness, etc.). Talk about your volunteer work or the ways you like to give back and/or help people. Talk about your biggest dream, how working for this company is part of that dream, and why you are passionate about it. Avoid any negative language (e.g., "I hate my old job").

Jot down some thoughts about the topics in the four points above.

Question 4: Why should we hire you?

Begin with what you believe the employer is looking for and explain how you fill that need. Talk about your personality traits and tell stories about your accomplishments that relate to the job description (using a story that links to the information is very powerful).

Example:

- Team player (linked to the team)

- Open and friendly to people (linked to customers)

- Driven and inspired to produce massive results (linked to managers)

- Creative and innovative (linked to engineers)

Question 5: What are your salary expectations?

This can be tricky because we tend to have a fear of asking for too much money, and we think we might lose the job, but no—you need to be bold and ask for the salary you deserve! Three out of five employees, on average, don't even negotiate the salary. And I can tell you that there is always money on the table and most companies try to lowball employees' salaries so they can save money. Regardless of whether the salary was mentioned in the job description or not, this strategy will apply.

To make it simple, you don't have to have an exact amount. Just know the range.

To do this, follow these steps.

Let's say you are applying to a project manager position at Facebook in California.

Step 1: Google "Project manager salaries in California" and "Facebook project manager salaries."

Step 2: You will find many resources: Glassdoor is a popular website for salary info. Now you have an idea of the range. Even if you can't find the company you are applying for, you can get a sense of what the salary ranges are in that type of position in that location or other similar companies.

Let's say the range is $100K–$120K.

Step 3: If you used to make something close to that, mention it. If not, you don't have to. Let's say you made $100K (you will not specify it, just the range).

Step 4: Go back to your long-term goals with the company that you jotted down in the previous section (relating your experience to the job description). "My plan is to stay with the company long-term and triple the department sales within the next three years."

Now let's add all of this together to create your answer. Here's a sample script you can use:

> I would like to be compensated fairly for my experience. My plan is to stay with the company long-term and triple the department sales within the next three years. I understand positions like this one pay in the range of $100K–$120K in our region. My previous salary was within that range, and with my type of experience, *I would like to receive something in the range of $110K–$130K, and it is negotiable.*

Now why did I say $110K–130K? Because you always want to give them a high anchor and work your way down. Otherwise you might lowball yourself.

I have a full section at the end in which I talk about salary negotiation in more detail, but this will be the general idea. Because it usually goes back and forth and sometimes you meet in the middle, I will explain how to do that.

Question 6: Why are you leaving/did you leave your job?

Here you want to focus on the future and what you plan to do for this company. Your reason for leaving (whether intentional or unintentional) should always be stated in a *positive* way. Avoid drama and negativity toward your previous employer.

Sample script:

> In my old job, I found myself limited in the position. The job was good, but I wanted more opportunities, challenges, and

diversity. I'm very passionate about this position and your company, and my goals are to produce amazing results, now and in the future. It's a big dream for me to start working here.

Write down some bullet points and use the sample script as a reference.

Question 7: **Why do you want this job?**

Here you talk about the job and, mostly, the company. This is where the research we did will pay off.

Talk about how passionate you are about the job, your goals, and your dreams.

- Use the research bullet points you collected in the previous section. This is where you talk about the company, its customers, and the products you like.

- Use the points you created for your greatest strengths. Talk about your qualifications for the job.

- Emphasize how you can add value to the company. Mention numbers, (e.g., profit increases), or if you don't have any experience, talk about a project you worked on previously at school, other jobs, etc.

Sample script:

I want this retail job because I'm very passionate about connecting with different people and using my expertise to satisfy their needs. I have a clear vision about my future with this company, and I am willing to put my heart and soul into the work I do. I love the company's mission because it aligns with my own, and I've followed their progress for years.

Use the four points and sample script to brainstorm some ideas.

Question 8: **How do you handle stress and pressure?**

Just give an example of how you handled stress and pressure and how they made you more productive. Make it short and sweet.

Question 9: **Describe a difficult work situation/project and how you overcame it.**

Share an example of what you did positively in a tough situation and what you decided to do to overcome this situation. You can use stories or examples. You want to come across as being confident and decisive.

Brainstorm some examples.

Question 10: **What are your goals for the future/Where do you see yourself in five years?**

Basically, here they want to know two things: 1) if you want to stay in the company or leave when you find a better opportunity, and 2) if your goals are aligned with the company's goals. You should show them that you are ambitious and hungry for the job and that you want to accomplish big things.

Step 1: Talk about how passionate you are about the job and the company and how your skills match the job requirements.

Step 2: Mention your short-term goals with the company. Example: "I want to be the best trainee in the three-month period."

Step 3: Mention your long-term goals with the company. Example: "Within three years, I want to go up to X position."

You have to know how the system of positions works in a company. For example: Engineering technician–Engineer 1–Engineer 2–Senior Engineer

If there is no clear direction (long- or short-term) for promotion from the position, talk about mastering that position and helping and teaching others your skills.

Sample Script:

Within three to five years, I will be an expert in my field. I will have developed close relationships with clients and expanded my client base, and my sales numbers will be among the top in the company.

2) Job title/company-specific interview questions

Now let's say you are applying for an electrical engineering job at Qualcomm.

There are three ways to get interview questions specific to the company and the position:

A) Job title interview questions

B) Company-specific interview questions

C) Company-specific and job title interview questions

You will do a Google search and type the following for each section:

A) "Electrical engineering interview questions"

B) "Qualcomm interview questions"

C) "Qualcomm electrical engineering interview questions"

You will find a lot of resources online: websites, courses, Glassdoor.com, YouTube videos, etc.

Compile 30–50 questions total (there will be a lot of ones repeated across the different websites).

You can use the STAR format we mentioned above and take from the ideas I mentioned for the top 10 generic questions. Remember to use summarized bullet points for each answer and make it very simple.

Now the interview questions are done! But there is the last and most important part. If you take away one thing from this chapter, it should be this: the most important aspect about interview preparation is one-on-one practice. You can do all the homework you want, but when you go in there and the nerves start to kick in, you can easily mess it all up because you didn't do the actual hands-on practice. It is just like warming up before lifting weights. If you don't do it, you may very well get injured.

Since you have all the questions and answered mapped out, start practicing one-on-one with someone you know who has great communication skills. To take it a step further, you can hire an interview coach who will give you quality feedback and help your improve your performance. Hence, reach out to me! You really need to practice numerous times before you can feel 100 percent confident. For some people, it comes naturally, while others struggle with it, but don't worry—with all the tools and strategies you've learned in this book, you will get there!

3. Logistics

After you do the one-on-one practice and feel ready for the interview, the last step will be to map out the logistics of the interview day.

1) **Dress code**

"Dress to impress" is what I always say to both ladies and gents. Wear something that makes you feel good. Research published in

July 2012 in the *Journal of Experimental Social Psychology* showed that dressing nicely makes you feel more confident and can drastically improve performance.

2) **Timing and technical details (Zoom, lighting, positioning, Wi-Fi connection)**

Make sure everything is ready. If it is a video call, check on all the details (Zoom, connection, lighting, etc.). If it is an in-person interview, make sure to arrive early to give yourself time to find the location, avoid traffic, etc.

3) **Review the interview success mindset section.**

Even if you do *zero* preparation and go in with a more powerful mindset, your performance will still be better than doing nothing.

4. The interview prep checklist

Now let's just add up all the previous sections into a simple checklist you can use before the interview.

1) Daily habits

    a) Make your bed

    b) Exercise

    c) Meditation

    d) Journaling

    e) Feed your mind something positive

2) Relating your experience to the job & company

    a) Relating your résumé to the job description

    b) Commonality points with the interviewers

    b) Studying the company

3) Interview questions

    a) The top 10 generic questions

    b) Job title/company-specific questions

4) Logistics

    a) Dress code

    b) Timing and technical details

    c) Review the interview success mindset

You're getting excited. You've done all your prep. You're hyped up for the interview. Maybe you're getting a bit nervous. The mental aspect is one part of the preparation, but you also want to do your homework as effectively as possible, because competence equals confidence. The more you're prepared, the more confident you'll be. It's one thing to keep your mind in shape and be positive, but it's another thing to come prepared. The more prepared you are, the calmer you will be.

Tomorrow is interview day! Let's put this checklist into a step-by-step action plan.

Let's say your interview is tomorrow at 3 p.m.

1.   Wake up at 7 a.m.

2.   Do the daily habits (Part 1 in the checklist)

3. Review your notes (Parts 2 and 3)

4. Review the logistics (Part 4)

In the final minutes before the actual interview, here's what I would like you to keep in mind. Number one, preparation is done; you did your part. Let everything go and look at the person interviewing you as a friend, someone you know. What does that mean? When you're talking to a friend, you speak from the heart and don't think about what you're going to say. You relax.

In the end, this person is not your enemy; they are on your side. They are just a normal human being with the same doubts and negative thoughts you have. They may be thinking, *Maybe this person doesn't think I'm good at interviewing. Did I ask the right questions?* Remember, this person is a friend you're going to build a natural organic relationship with. Be yourself, ask them questions, and be interested in getting to know them on a personal level. This is very, very important.

The second part is to detach completely from the outcome of this interview, which means whatever happens, happens. You go in and do your best. You cannot control what the company will decide. If this works out, great. If not, there are many other fish in the sea, and this one is just not meant to be. You will get other opportunities if this doesn't work out. It's not the end of the world, and you will not die. You can move on and find more interviews and other companies.

I've seen it happen many times in two scenarios: in Scenario 1, my client is pumped and ready, having major expectations that things will work out. They go in thinking they nailed it and end up with a rejection letter. In Scenario 2, my client goes in with zero expectations, feeling they did horrible, and then they end up getting an offer.

I learned how the power of having zero expectations can really ease the pressure, and the more relaxed you are, the better you will perform.

I've talked a lot about being in the abundance mindset. In this case, it simply means that not only is the company interviewing you, but you are also interviewing *them*. Maybe you will like them, maybe you won't. Just because they give you a paycheck, that doesn't mean that they have power over you. You, in the end, are in control and get to choose what's best for you.

After the first round, make sure to always follow up with the recruiter or hiring manager for feedback and to collect information on how to prepare for the next round. Remember that your relationship with every person in the interview is extremely important to grow and maintain, because if you do a good job and they like you, even if you didn't get that specific position, there is always an opportunity for another position.

Let me tell you the story of one of my clients, Jessica. Jessica was a great project manager with more than 15 years of experience. Within the first two weeks of our working together, she was getting a lot of interviews, and she was overwhelmed. Within a week, she had three interviews at her top companies. She nailed the first two, but the last one didn't go so well. Long story short, she ended up getting rejected by the first two companies and actually got an offer from the third one, where she felt she had done the worst.

The whole job application process is a numbers game. It's similar to dating: you date multiple people, but only one or two of them will like you and things will work out. It's the same with interviews or offers. You will go through failed interviews, and you will go through failed offers. It's a part of the game. Don't take it personally when you do get faced with rejection and failure.

Salary Negotiation

You nailed the interviews and you're at the last stages of negotiating the salary. What do you need to do next? In the top 10 generic interview questions section, I briefly explained how to answer the question "What are your salary expectations?" That will get you started, but the real negotiations start when you receive the offer letter in your email. But before we get into that, let's do a quick recap of that question.

Let's say you are applying to a project manager position at Facebook in California.

Step 1: Google "Project manager salaries in California" and "Facebook project manager salaries."

Step 2: You will find many resources: Glassdoor is a popular website for salary info. Now you have an idea of the range. Even if you can't find the company you are applying for, you can get a sense of what the salary ranges are in that type of position in that location or other similar companies.

Let's say the range is $100K–$120K.

Step 3: If you used to make something close to that, mention it. If not, you don't have to. Let's say you made $100K (you will not specify it, just the range).

Step 4: Go back to your long-term goals with the company that you jotted down in the previous section (relating your experience to the job description). "My plan is to stay with the company long-term and triple the department sales within the next three years."

Now let's add all of this together to create your answer. Here's a sample script you can use:

> I would like to be compensated fairly for my experience. My plan is to stay with the company long-term and triple the department sales within the next three years. I understand positions like this one pay in the range of $100K–$120K in our region. My previous salary was within that range, and with my type of experience, *I would like to receive something in the range of $110K–$130K, and it is negotiable.*

The most common fear for all people who get a new job is: "If I negotiate for a higher salary, I might lose the job." This is totally not true! When you negotiate for a higher salary, this puts you in a position of *power* and shows the employer that you are confident and will be a very valuable asset to the company. I work with my clients on this all the time, and every single one of them who got an offer negotiated for a higher salary and got it. How do you get a higher salary? It's actually very simple.

It comes down to three things:

1) Build your case. You will need to prove you are worth investing in, with specific examples of value you've given to employers in your career.

2) Face some resistance. Even airtight cases for a salary increase can face resistance, so be prepared to answer questions, especially, "Why do you deserve this salary?"

3) Strike a balance between firm and flexible. Your salary negotiations won't go well if you refuse to give any ground or say yes to a minimal

salary increase. Be prepared to go back and forth during negotiations, and be sure that any compromise reached is acceptable.

Let's say you got an offer of $110K (the range we used in the example is $110K–$130K).

Step 1: Don't accept the offer right away. Tell them you need time to think about it.

Step 2: Set up a call with the recruiter or hiring manager to discuss the offer. Before hopping on that call, make sure to do the daily habits so you are in a stronger frame of mind. Also, conduct this call while standing up tall and strong (that will help with your tone of voice and confidence).

The plan is to ask for **$120K** ($10K more than what they offered). Why, you think? Well, why not? These companies make millions of dollars every year, and you deserve a part of that. Also, look at how hard you've worked to get to this point in your life—all the years of schooling, the hard work, the obstacles you had to go through–to be standing tall and proud here today. You deserve what you're worth.

Now you are thinking, *Okay, how can I pitch $120K confidently?*

First, remember that there are multiple parts to the offer:

1) Base salary

2) Compensation package (stock options, PTO, medical/dental/vision insurance, retirement savings plan, etc.)

3) Bonuses (performance, annual, profit sharing, sign-up, retention, referrals, holiday, noncash, project based, commission)

Now each company is different, and you want to make sure you fully understand the offer letter and all the details of what's included.

We will start by asking for a higher base ($120K) and then tap into the other two options (comp package and bonuses) if needed.

Let's start here: first of all, mention the highest range from the research that you did, then think about what goals you are hungry to accomplish for this company and what you are willing to do (think big). What are you proud of from your experience, past projects, and what you've accomplished? I want you to brag and be *confident*. That's what they are looking for! You want to *really* show them your overall enthusiasm about their company and the new position.

Sample script:

> Hey James/Jessica. I just reviewed the offer, and I am excited about this opportunity. I'm very enthusiastic about the position and the company. As I mentioned before, I'm thinking more long-term and hope to accomplish XYZ. I've researched the industry we are in and the current market value. Given my qualifications and experience, I would be most comfortable accepting a salary of $120K for this role.

Step 3: Now they will counter with one of the following: 1) they will offer you the $120K, 2) they will offer you a lower amount, or 3) it will be a take-it-or-leave-it type of situation. For 2 and 3, here is what you can do.

Tap into the other parts of the offer (compensation package and bonuses).

> Hey James/Jessica, if we can't get a higher base salary due to the budget, what about get an extra (bonus, stock option, etc.) that will get me up to $120K total?

You literally want to keep fighting until the end. Hold your ground and be strong. It's normal to face resistance sometimes.

Step 4: Now they will come back to you with a final decision. If it's an increase, just accept it. If they don't offer anything more, ask them why they didn't (maybe they have a budget). After that, you will decide if you are willing to accept the offer and move on or not. And that's it!

Let me share a quick story of one my clients, Paul. Paul landed a three-month contract-to-hire role at an amazing company. They started with a $165K salary and promised him it would go up to $200K if they decided to hire him full-time. Three months passed, and they decided to give him the full-time position because his performance was amazing and they loved him.

The recruiter came back with an offer letter, but the salary stayed at $165K. When he called me, he was excited, and he was about to accept it because he really loved the company and didn't care too much about the salary. I told him "No!" He talked to the recruiter, and she came back with "Oh, it's a budgeting thing" and wasn't nice about it at all. I told him, "Forget about the recruiter. Set up a call with the hiring manager directly and simply ask him for what you truly want, which is the $200K!"

Even the hiring manager was resistant, but I practiced with Paul and taught him to stand his ground. Finally, he ended up getting the $200K he wanted!

So you see, if you don't ask for what you want, they will simply lowball you and give you the lowest salary possible. Don't miss out on the opportunity to get a better salary. You deserve it!

Suzan was in the final stages of negotiating her offer, and the hiring manager asked her, "What kind of salary would you like?" She used to make $100K, and she I practiced pitching $115K, even though she was terrified to do it.

She gathered all the courage she had and finally asked for $115K. The manager came back with "Oh, that's it? I thought you were going to ask me for $120K. I was thinking around that number!" She was shocked. If she had asked for $120K, she would have gotten it, but also, if she hadn't asked for anything, they were going to give her $100K because she had told them that's what she used to make!

So you see, there is *always* money on the table. If you don't ask for it, you'll miss out on the chances of getting an amazing salary!

After you negotiate the salary and have a start date for the job, this can be your plan moving forward.

How to Build a Strong Foundation when Starting Your Dream Job

THE WEEKEND BEFORE YOU START

1. What are my goals with the company?

2. With my team/boss?

   a. Build a strong relationship with them

   b. Get to know their network

3. With their products and services?

4. Short-term?

5. Long-term?

FIRST DAY

1. My team: Who is working on your team? (Managers, engineers, sales, assistants, secretaries, upper management)

    a. John (engineer) same team

    b. James (manager) co-op team

    c. Kacey (assistant manager)

    d. Jeff (sales)

2. Build a commonality list for each person

3. Products and services: How does everything work?

4. Familiarize yourself with the company website, training materials, etc.

5. Prepare yourself mentally and physically every day: daily habits

MID-WEEK

1. Post your job on LinkedIn and Facebook. Show people your enthusiasm for the new job.

2. Grab lunch or coffee with one or two of your teammates. Start to build a social circle.

END OF THE WEEK

1. Take notes of what happened throughout the week.

2. Set up a check-in meeting with your boss.

3. Talk to them about your first week, show your enthusiasm, and confirm you are meeting expectations.

4. Start to build a relationship with them.

Overall

1. Help teammates with tasks as much as you can.

2. Learn from the key players/upper-level people in the company. Find

out who's doing the best in the company and build a relationship with them. Make them your mentor.

3. If you think some things could be changed or done better, communicate that to your team/manager.

4. Innovate. When given tasks, take the initiative to come up with ideas for doing things better. Think outside the box. When given tasks, most employees jump into them right away, but you need to work smarter, not harder. Ask "How can I do this better and faster?" and then have the courage to advance and implement the ideas

5. Collaborate. Ask "How can I help others succeed?" When your team wins, you win along with them. It's not all about you. When you're a team player, you build a strong foundation for your own success. According to Mehta, "Who gets credit is irrelevant. What matters is that as a team you are doing great work, achieving your goals. Steer people in the right direction. Make others look good— your clients, colleagues, bosses, and employees. Be a true team player and success will come back to you tenfold."

6. When your boss asks you something and you don't know the answer, Google it. Become a researching machine.

7. Chase skills, not titles. People get so focused on what they *should* do that they lose sight of what they *could* do. Your success in the long run won't come from working for a dream company or holding a prestigious job title. It depends on the skills and abilities you learn and bring to the table.

8. Just like competing in a sporting competition, your overall performance is dependent on three things:

a) Do what all the other employees won't do: if you need to work weekends, do it.

b) Maintain a positive attitude, no matter what happens.

c) Commit to growth and contribution.

9. Don't make your job your life. Other than being a top performer in the company, think about what matters most to you: your family and friends, hobbies, and passions. While you're busy and going through your week, remember to always make time for these other priorities.

And that's it! Congratulations on getting your dream job! Use this section as a cheat sheet and read it every week on Sunday for five minutes to remind yourself of how to continuously grow and thrive in the company.